4

40388

13
A5

HOW TO BE A
WRITER

HOW TO BE A WRITER

Copyright © Stewart Ferris, 2005

First published 2005

Reprinted 2005, 2006 and 2007

This revised edition published 2013 by Summersdale Publishers Ltd.

Summersdale Publishers Ltd
46 West Street
Chichester
West Sussex
PO19 1RP
UK

www.summersdale.com

Printed and bound by CPI Group (UK) Ltd, Croydon, CR0 4YY

ISBN: 978-1-84953-345-4

Substantial discounts on bulk quantities of Summersdale books are available to corporations, professional associations and other organisations. For details contact Nicky Douglas by telephone: +44 (0) 1243 756902, fax +44 (0) 1243 786300 or email: nicky@summersdale.com.

HOW TO BE A WRITER

Secrets from the Inside

Stewart Ferris

summersdale

AUTHOR'S NOTE

This book has been constructed upon the foundations of its successful previous edition. The publishing and media industries are changing rapidly, and this expanded book (more than twice as long as the original) brings the subject up to date and encompasses additional themes based on topics raised by the hundreds of readers who contacted me in recent years with questions about their own writing. Thank you to everyone who took the trouble to email me with feedback and ideas, and I hope this new work will help the next generation of creative-minded people to become the writers they want to be.

CONTENTS

FOREWORD

*'A writer is a person for whom writing is more
difficult than it is for other people.'*
Thomas Mann

I am many things. I'm a husband. A pedestrian. A consumer.
A son. A graduate. A driver. A viewer. A Cicestrian (look it up).
A publisher. A rubbish marathon runner. A pain in the neck. But
I don't usually define myself by those labels. I call myself a writer.
That isn't to say that I spend the majority of my time engaged in
that pursuit. It's not unknown for me to scribble for fewer hours in
a day than I squander under the hypnotic glow of the television, but
on official forms I describe myself as a writer, not a couch potato.

What does it mean to be a writer? A storyteller, perhaps? A
literary exhibitionist? A recorder of the human experience? It
sounds rather splendid and noble, but it isn't how I regard myself.
My chosen trade surrounds me with frustration and torment.

It's a peculiar calling. I quietly yearn for a life free of the
shackles of my creative streak. My somewhat tragic fantasy is to
be able to spend a day doing nothing and not suffer the inevitable
remorse that feels like lead in my stomach. But whenever a whole
day passes without any words making it from my head to my
word processor, the shame becomes entrenched. It's exasperating.
Maddening.

I've called myself a writer since Lady Di haircuts and leg
warmers were the height of fashion, although I haven't actually
been a writer during every one of those intervening years. Some
years would go by with no creative output at all. Others would
see plays, books, songs, sitcoms, or other literary products taking
shape. Some went nowhere other than the filing cabinet (and later,

the virtual filing cabinet of the computer); others saw publication, production or recording. By age 15 I had a folder crammed full of ideas for books, plays and films that I wanted to write, and almost thirty years later I still have that folder and I still haven't had time to work on them. It doesn't really matter now: I think the time for topical satires about Thatcher's Britain and sketches written for Frankie Howerd may have passed. But the failure to complete the unrealistic mountain of ideas for writing projects I had in my youth is yet another source of irrational regret.

For those fortunate enough not to be afflicted by this curse of creativity it's probably hard to conceive what it feels like. Try to imagine you're a teenager about to go to bed having failed to tackle your school homework, and you know the teacher's going to make you regret your laziness the next day. It feels a bit like that. Conversely, at the end of a productive literary day an endorphin rush floods me in a tsunami of satisfaction. There's no greater sensation than knowing a writing project has taken a giant leap towards completion. That's the positive force that motivates me to write.

Being a writer is emotionally tough. It's a self-punishing existence demanding anti-social hours and rarely paying a return that bears any relation to the eons spent perfecting the craft. So why did I become a writer? A moment to ponder the horror of what it would mean for me to be anything else should answer that. When I worked in a yogurt factory I had to quit within a week because the rubber gloves made the skin of my hands peel off. When I was a pizza waiter I made Basil Fawlty look competent. When I was a book sales representative I used to spend more money buying all the irresistible new publications in Waterstones than I made from selling them. I'm just not cut out to be anything other than a writer.

Fortunately I happen to be extremely skilled at sitting on a chair. I hardly ever fall off. I also have a basic competence at the task of rearranging words that I find lying around in the dictionary, not to mention the ability to press clearly labelled buttons on a keyboard. I was born for this role. But, of course, it wasn't that easy. Nurturing a book from idea to completion can take years. Developing the literary skills to make it publishable can take decades. When I look up at my bookcase and see my own books filling an entire shelf, I thank my younger self for having had the courage to build something for my future. The results of a day's literary labours will still be visible long after a day I squandered lounging around unproductively has been forgotten. I sense a timeline stretching ahead of me, like a conveyor belt into the future. Writing is like putting a gift on that conveyor belt, knowing that it will help my future self.

If you dream of one day putting 'writer' on official paperwork, the effort starts now. Write something each day for the benefit of your future self. Make yourself proud. Anyone can be a writer if they want to, but to make the transition from being a 'waitress who writes' to plain 'writer' requires a commitment to work with the person you are now and the person you're going to become. There's no switch, no magic wand that can transform you instantly. You need to accept the downside of this vocation: the quotidian guilt that accompanies failure to make as much progress as you would like. But only by embracing that pain can you reward yourself in later life with the fruits of your endeavours. And in truth, it's the guilt that we feel when we don't write that defines us as writers more strongly than the words that we actually do write. If it doesn't bother you that you've written nothing all week, I would question whether you really are going to be a writer. If you're frustrated by your recent lack of creative progress, excellent. We can work together on this. Read on: this book is for you.

LET'S BEGIN

To become a writer it's not enough just to write. Everyone does that. Emails, texts, Facebook posts, letters of complaint to the local newspaper – but those people don't want to be writers. You do. You have to become something different. Something special. You have to learn not only how to write, but how to destroy sentences that you've lovingly crafted. You'll need to delete paragraphs, throw away chapters, or even whole books or scripts. Being a writer is not about writing. It's about rewriting. Improving. Starting again. Polishing. Honing your skill. Learning from those who are better than you. Recognising your own mistakes and weaknesses. Developing critical judgement. Some rather unpleasantly describe the requisite skills as the ability to 'murder your babies'. It's a horrible phrase, but there's no denying that self-editing can be an unsavoury experience. I prefer a more positive way of looking at it: being a writer means accepting nothing less than a joyous symphony of perfectly arranged words.

Time for a reality check. This bit might knock your confidence to the floor, and if so, I apologise, but don't worry – I'm going to help you build it back up during the course of this book.

I just need to purge you of any misconceptions and ideals early on because they won't help you in the long run. Do you really think your first full screenplay will tempt someone to make it into a film? Is your first completed novel good enough to be published? I know as a writer that your instinctive reaction is to say 'Of course it's good enough'. After the thousands of hours you've put into writing it, how could it not be? Everything I've ever written has always seemed perfect to me. At first. With the perspective and objectivity of passing time, I always come back to a project with fresh eyes and see its faults. Nothing is ever as perfect as it seems when you write the first draft. Even if it's the tenth draft of your first book, it's unlikely to be as good as the tenth draft of your second book.

Improvement as a writer is not optional – it's unavoidable. It means what you write first is not as good, literate, marketable, enjoyable, readable or satisfyingly huggable as your second project. The stories you proudly wrote at school are laughably bad in the adult world. You got better, and you'll keep getting better. If you put in the hours, you'll eventually reach the point at which your writing can be considered to be of a professional standard. You will have found your 'voice'. You will have matured in the way you create sentences and structure the flow of ideas. And you'll understand why your early works are best left on your computer hard drive, unread. You'll also realise that those abandoned projects were essential steps in reaching the giddy literary heights that you now occupy. Don't regret the time spent on lengthy writing projects that no one reads. They helped to get you where you are now. But that's all they will ever be.

To become the writer you want to be there's something else you'll need: inspiration. Ideas. Creative juices. Again, everyone has ideas. We writers don't have the monopoly on inspiration. But it's up to us to do something with the random thoughts that lodge themselves in our heads from time to time. More importantly, we have to develop the ability to find inspiration when it seems lacking. We have to put ourselves into the right physical environment and a suitable frame of mind to permit our brains to fill with gushing waterfalls of ideas. I'll explain how to achieve all of those things in this book. I will also show how it's possible and even desirable to write without waiting for inspiration to descend upon you, lights flashing, angels singing with stories handed to you from the cosmos on a silver plate. Because I know that such events can be tricky to concoct and can't always be guaranteed.

This book is for all writers, in all genres, but most of the examples apply to book writers because they form the biggest single group. The pain we all experience in trying to put words on the page is the same whatever the genre, however. This book presupposes only that you want to be a writer. No previous experience is necessary. I'll take you through all aspects of what it takes to be a professional writer in the publishing and media industries today. There are some harsh truths exposed in this book and many myths will be shattered. The reality of writing is not what many people believe it to be. Some of these chapters may surprise or disappoint you.

My aim in revealing the secrets of the writing game is not to destroy your ambitions and dreams, but to empower you to be able to achieve them.

Read this book before embarking on a career as a writer. Use it to inspire you to achieve high standards, greatness and professionalism. Without those you have nothing. With them you can conquer the literary world.

The Success Pyramid

The community of writers who can command a living wage from their work is very small. That's the community you want to join. How many people are knocking on the doors looking for space in that community just like you?

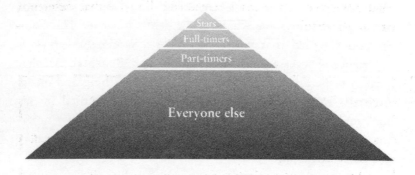

The top group consists of the superstar authors, the lucky and talented few who have made it rich through their writing. This group includes J. K. Rowling, Stephen King, Bill Bryson and anyone else who has managed to turn their name into a saleable brand that can command high advances.

The second group from the top is a little larger, and consists of all those writers who are able to earn enough from their writing not to need to do any other work. Most of them are not at all famous or glamorous, just jobbing authors who scrape enough successes to pay the mortgage and feed the dog.

The third group from the top consists of writers who earn some money from writing, but not enough to be able to write full-time. They might have had one or two books published with moderate success, or they might sell the odd article or television script. Many are happy where they are, though some would prefer to move up a level so they could earn enough from writing to be able to tell their bosses where to stick their jobs.

And the giant group at the bottom is everyone else. The many millions who have yet to earn any money from writing and who dream of finding a shortcut straight to the top of the pyramid. Little do they realise that there's only one difference between them and the fortunate people higher up who earn money from writing. It's a difference that is easily remedied. I'll reveal that difference later in this book.

Top tips for budding writers

- Writers need to be prepared to delete their words as well as create them.
- A completed first draft is not a completed work.
- Writers improve throughout their lives.
- Bad writing is a stepping stone towards good writing.

1

PREPARATION FOR BEING A WRITER

TOOLS OF THE TRADE

Let's start with the basics. A writer needs to communicate their thoughts into written words, and there are four main methods of achieving this:

Writing longhand with a pen and paper

Produce a draft using a pen and paper, then type it onto a word processor. This has an inherent advantage of forcing you to review and rewrite your initial efforts, so the first version to appear on your computer is actually a second draft. The pen is not an alternative to a computer; it's just an additional step that some writers prefer.

If you write longhand, don't skimp on the pen and paper. You'll be scribbling hundreds or even thousands of words a day as a writer so it's vital to choose a pen that is comfortable to hold and that can get the ink quickly enough onto the paper to enable you to write at full speed when the ideas are flowing.

Choose a notebook that makes your writing feel special. Look in the stationery shop for a notebook that inspires you. There are blank notebooks that look like bound hardback books, or you may be more inspired by spiral-bound journalists' pads. But don't fall into the trap of buying a notebook that is so beautiful you feel that to write anything inside it would spoil it. The real beauty will come from your words, your doodles, your notes. This notebook will be your first draft, not your final draft, so don't be afraid to explore your creativity even if half of what you write ends up in a literary dead-end and never makes it onto the typed version.

Typing directly into a computer

Any computer on the market today is more than adequate for word-processing work. Word processing is the least demanding of all major computer applications, so the only relevant factor in choosing a computer to write with is whether you want a laptop or a desktop.

If your writing base is at home and in a private, consistently quiet area, a desktop computer will be best. They're available with larger screens: I have dual screens, and one of them is turned to a portrait position, giving me the ability to see up to 1,500 words of my book at a time when I'm writing. But if you want the flexibility to write in other locations, a laptop will give you that freedom. Battery life varies, but most will give three to six hours of power before warning you to save and close your work before they shut down. If there's mains power available you can run the laptop from that, and in some long-haul airline cabins you can even plug your laptop in to the seat for in-flight power.

Laptops have less space for keyboards, so the keys are smaller and closer together. This isn't a problem for typing once you get used to it. In fact, the reduced distance your fingers have to cover can actually speed up typing. The only difficulty comes when switching from a laptop keyboard to a desktop keyboard and adjusting to the change.

Tablets such as the iPad have virtual keyboards which are not ideal as your primary method of input unless you are extremely patient or nimble of finger, although I've seen many would-be wordsmiths tapping determinedly at their tablets in coffee houses, and on planes and trains. It's plainly a keyboard skill that can be mastered. The iPhone and other smartphones also have word-processing functionality, but the virtual keyboard is so small that the speed and reliability (hitting the right key every time is beyond the ability of my chubby digits) of input make it suitable for occasional use only.

Using dictation software

If you prefer talking to typing, why not give dictation software a try? It will transcribe your voice into text in a word-processing document. In theory this is a great idea, giving all of us the opportunity to write like Dame Barbara Cartland used to do, laid back on a chaise longue dictating masterpieces without ever having to type. I met the famously pink-bedecked Barbara Cartland at a book launch party a couple of years before she died. Our conversation was problematic to say the least: she was too deaf to hear me and her voice was too soft for me to hear her. Quite how her dictation secretary used to cope, I've no idea. The problem with dictation software is actually very similar to that of trying to converse with a deaf ninety-six-year-old surrounded by noisy, drunk publishers. The words get misinterpreted, and the resultant prose can be gibberish. But it's possible to train the software to get used to your voice, and eventually you should get to the stage where the computer can truly be said to 'understand' you. Give it a go if you think it will help you to write. I tried it briefly, but if someone else is within earshot it seems strange to be talking to your computer (although shouting at it in frustration is not generally regarded as being out of the ordinary).

Using a typewriter

If you view the process of typing your work on a typewriter as the equivalent of writing longhand, then fine. Type it once on paper then type it again into a computer. If you think that typing on a typewriter will generate the final product, you're wrong. That isn't how the publishing and media industries work these days. Everything has to be processed through a computer, and if you can only supply your writing on photocopied sheets then you're adding unnecessary costs for the publisher because if they want to accept your work someone will have to re-key every word of it. Scanning using optical character recognition software is a possibility for them, but it's slow and unreliable and will add mistakes to your work. Typewritten work will only be tolerated from established authors (usually of a very senior age).

Don't put yourself at a disadvantage at the start of your writing career by not bothering to learn how to use a computer. If you want to have a chance of being regarded as a professional writer, use a computer.

TYPING SKILLS

Are you one of those writers who object to using a computer on the grounds that they don't know how to type? Really? You mean you're incapable of looking at a printed letter on a button and pressing it? I don't know how to type, and I've probably typed over three million words onto computers. Of course, typing the first book was slow. I had to look at what my fingers were doing. I took no typing lessons. I just used one finger on one hand and one finger on the other, and roughly divided the keyboard between them. Typing the second book was a little quicker. Occasionally I could take my eyes off the keyboard and still hit the right key. That was a nice feeling, but I couldn't rely on it. I started using two fingers from each hand on the next few books to speed things up a little. Several books later came the revelation that I wasn't looking at the keyboard any more. I never noticed the moment of transition, but somehow I reached a point at which I only needed to look at the screen while my four typing fingers managed to hit all the right keys. I think I now use about three fingers on each hand for typing, but my fingers move so fast I can't really tell. One thing's certain: I can type a lot faster than I can write with a pen and I only look at the keyboard to find the punctuation keys.

Fast typing generates errors, known in the business as 'typos'. They are a normal part of writing and can be easily fixed during later rewrites. The first draft of this book contained plenty of typos, but they only took a short time to fix using my computer. Imagine if I'd typed the book on a typewriter: to insert a few words into one paragraph on a typewriter used to require typing out the entire page again. With the two or three mistakes per page that were present in the first draft of this book I'd have had to retype the whole thing, which would be like rebuilding a house just because a bulb had blown. At least with the computer I can make repairs to individual words and the rest of the paragraph layout adjusts accordingly.

Did my eagle-eyed editor spot the typos that I missed?[1] Let me know via the email address on my website if any slipped through the net!

66 *If my doctor told me I had only six minutes to live, I wouldn't brood. I'd type a little faster.* 99

Isaac Asimov

---

1 American readers please note that I've written this book in British English, so you might think something is wrong when actually it's just a different way of spelling a word to the one you're used to. In particular, we Brits are less keen on the letter 'z' (pronounced 'zed', not 'zee', of course) than you are, so please don't be offended by such apparent spelling atrocities as 'recognise' or 'monetise'.

BACKUPS

There's nothing more frustrating than typing into your computer a page of exquisite text that you're convinced is going to make you the next Thomas Hardy, only to find that it all disappears into the ether the moment your neighbour's DIY project causes a blackout in the street. Don't trust technology. Don't even trust paper. Floods and fires do happen (sadly not often at the same time). Back up everything you write every day. Hard disks fail. USB memory sticks disappear like biros. Files can get corrupted. Save after every paragraph you type into a computer – otherwise you could lose pages of work if there's a power cut (unless you're working on a laptop).

When writing by hand, photocopy every page. Keep copies at different locations.

If you're writing whilst travelling, email your documents to yourself or post photocopies back home.

In addition to the manual kinds of backup, subscribe to a 'cloud' storage service. I have several of these – there's one that comes as part of my anti-virus software, another that I pay for specifically, and another that helps my iPhone talk to my desktop. I also recently began using Dropbox, which copies my documents onto all of my devices as well as storing them up in the sky somewhere. The service is free up to a certain amount of data (it's more than sufficient for text documents) and has proved to be so reliable for me that I no longer email files to myself or bother using memory sticks to transfer my work. Visit www.stewartferris.com for links to Dropbox and other backup solutions. You can't have too many of these things. Belt and braces, as it's known. Your work is precious and deserves the best protection you can find.

❝ *Writing is not a job description.*
A great deal of it is luck. **❞**

MARGARET ATWOOD

SHOULD YOU GIVE UP
THE DAY JOB?

You're all set up as a writer now, so go ahead. Resign. In a week or two you'll get an advance for your sample chapter that pays off the mortgage and buys you a holiday home in the south of France, right?

Wrong. Firstly, an unknown writer won't get an advance for a sample chapter[2]. How does the publisher know you can continue writing at that quality until the end of the book? How do they know your rip-roaring story won't fizzle out in a few chapters? The best-case scenario would be an encouraging letter or email saying they like the sample and would be happy to look at the finished book when it's ready. No commitment. No money. Months later, when you've finished the book and sent it to them, you will then have to wait weeks for a reply. Sometimes months. If they make an offer to publish, you still won't see any of that advance until the contract is signed, and even then you'll only receive a portion of it (the rest is reserved for when the book is published, probably 18 months later).

So your payment might be as much as two years away, and that's if you're fortunate enough to get an offer from the first publisher you send it to. Will that royalty advance change your life? Enormous advances hit the headlines, so understandably that's what you think you'll get. But 99 per cent of publishing deals don't involve huge sums of cash. An average advance in the industry is unlikely to buy you a new sofa let alone a new house. The dilution of the publishing world that followed the dramatic

---

2 I was contacted by a reader of the first edition of this book who, rather irritatingly, has proven me wrong on this score. She wrote ten pages, an agent loved it and sparked a bidding war amongst publishers eager to sign her up, and she is now a Penguin author. Her success story breaks all the rules. It's amazing and impressive. But it's the exception. Don't assume it will happen to you because it's not what happens to most writers! I'll explain more about the mechanics of getting published later in this book, but for now we're going to focus on the process of writing.

success of eBooks and the ease and affordability of digital self-publishing has resulted in even lower advances as publishers attempt to shield themselves from competition that seems to grow exponentially. You'll still be able to buy a sofa with your advance, but these days it's likely to be from the charity shop.

The cynical side of me would therefore say that the best way to make a living as a writer is to get another job (or keep the one you have already). But I know it doesn't have to be that way. There has to be room for dreams and ambitions. You write because you have the imagination and creativity to make something out of nothing. If you have the power to perform such alchemy, the ability to monetise your output must be within your grasp. Just don't do anything to harm your original source of income until you have proven that not only can you replace it with cash derived from writing but that you can do so consistently.

An example of the timescale involved in receiving money from a publisher

Year 1	
Jan	Write a sample chapter
Feb	Polish sample and send to publisher
Mar	Continue writing more chapters while waiting for response
Apr	Publisher requests to see the rest of the book
May	Writing and re-writing
Jun	Finish book and send to publisher
Jul – Aug	Waiting for a response
Sep	Offer arrives from publisher
Oct	Contract is negotiated and signed
Nov	One half of the advance is received
Dec	Publisher requests rewrites
Year 2	
Jan	Writing
Feb	Submit rewrites
Mar – Sep	Waiting
Oct	Publication date
Nov	Second half of advance is received

THINK LIKE A WRITER

The disadvantage of being a writer is the necessity to read actively and watch actively. Non-writers can read and be entertained passively. The magic and joy of being entertained in blissful ignorance of how that medium of entertainment was developed and delivered to you will disappear forever once you train yourself to think like a writer.

The simplest example of this is in the world of comedy. I've known comedy writers who had become incapable of laughter. When someone told them a joke they merely considered it for a moment, then nodded their heads and mumbled, 'Very good, yes, that works'. It wasn't because they had no sense of humour, it was just that they didn't permit their minds to accept the surprise factor that normally triggers the laughter response: instead of laughing they analysed how that joke was constructed and whether it could have been done better. By learning different humorous formulae they are able to make new jokes themselves using the same structure.

When you next read a novel, think about the structure of the story and the way the subplot weaves around the main plot. Think about what the writer is telling you directly and what is being hinted at. Think about the length of the chapter, the length of the paragraphs, the style of the dialogue. Think about the amount of descriptive detail compared to the amount of action taking place. Think about how the writer is moving the story forwards, maintaining pace and interest, making you want to keep reading. You think this would ruin the story for you? Too right. But it has to be done. Do you think a magician is amazed by his own tricks? Of course not, because he knows how they work. Only the passive audience enjoys it. It's the same with writing. Once you deconstruct someone's writing in order to see how they did it you cease to belong to the fictional world of that story and you're just a cynical outsider counting the number of adjectives in the opening scene.

When you watch a sitcom or a movie or a cartoon, think about the structure. Try to identify scenes, acts and twists and turns in the plot. Look for moments where the character develops into something deeper than they were at the beginning. Note the balance between action scenes and slow-paced scenes. See how minimal the dialogue is and how much is said without words by use of expression, symbolism, movement and music. Think about whether the characters are talking directly about the plot or whether the story is moving forward as a subtle undertone in a dialogue that's heavily pregnant with dual meaning.

This is what it means to think like a writer. You're going to be a professional, someone who knows the tricks of the trade, the inside secrets that allow only a small number of people to make a successful career from their words. Keep that frame of mind the whole time. Live and breathe the concept of being a writer and thinking like a writer. Active reading and viewing will seem strange and uncomfortable at first. It's only natural: you're taking that red pill and leaving the matrix of polished entertainment forever. You're about to enter the real world where you need to get behind the scenes and understand the commercial side of the industry. Writing is the backbone of all media and you can join the elite few who get paid to provide those words for the rest of us.

DRESS LIKE A WRITER

Go on, if it helps you to get into the role. What does a writer wear, though? Probably not the smart suit you wore to work, so take that off for a start. I'm wearing jeans and a roll-neck sweater while I'm writing this because it's comfy and it doesn't really matter what I look like when I write because no one's watching me. Besides, it keeps me warm while I sit idly for hours on end and saves on heating bills. Writing naked is something to aspire to if your climate permits, which regrettably in my case it rarely does. The process of writing a book is one thing they haven't made a reality television show out of yet, thank goodness, so it will never matter what you look like when writing. If it helps, you can buy a hat with 'writer' on it. Each to their own.

IS IT GLAMOROUS?

Of course. Launch parties, signing sessions, television interviews, autographs in the street. How could the lifestyle of a successful working author be anything other than the epitome of glamour?

Actually, it isn't. Take a moment to visualise being an author at the top of the heap. Everyone is buying your books. You're the toast of the literary world. You're able to write full-time because you're earning so much in royalties. But what does a typical year hold for you? How much of the glamour will you actually experience? When your new bestseller is released there will be one launch party which lasts for about three hours. You will then spend one hectic month touring the country visiting bookshops to sign copies for your fans, interspersed with some local radio interviews and the occasional mad dash back to the capital for television interviews. And the price of this one month of apparent glamour? Eleven months locked in a shed on your own, writing, rewriting, rewriting again, and then again. And again. Etc. And when your month of glamour ends, it's back to your shed to spend the next eleven months working on the follow-up book.

Writing suits solitary people. It's not for those who value drinking with their friends in the pub every night above all other pleasures. Some kinds of writing, such as comedy and non-fiction, are suited to writing teams of two or more. But it's more likely that you'll be on your own in your struggle to prove to the world that you can write, so you'll need to motivate yourself.

Pick up your pen right now, hold it high in the air and shout 'I can do it! I will be a writer!' Now apologise to the librarian.

Reader's question:
I want to get into the writing
industry. What should I do?

From a pedantic point of view, I could argue that you're already in it. If you're reading this book, it's more than likely that you've already attempted some creative writing or are about to do so. That's precisely where everyone in this business starts (not with my book, sadly, but with writing something). But what the question really means is how to turn those words into an income, how to achieve that paradigm shift from amateur to professional. It feels like there's an invisible barrier, difficult to penetrate, bouncing your submitted words back at you with callous rejection notes. Generating cash from words typed into a computer can seem an impossibility from outside that protective force field. But every author now earning a living or a partial living from their work had to break in to the industry somehow. And that choice of phrase is rather revealing: 'break in'. It's as if there's no clearly defined, honest entrance to the industry and the only way in is to smash your way through its defences.

Think about what the 'writing industry' actually consists of. It's not a homogenous, unified business. It doesn't have many career openings for which you can train, qualify and step in to. The writing industry is a fragmented and hugely varied world, consisting of poets, journalists, novelists, travel writers, biographers, technical writers, academic writers, playwrights, screenwriters, comedy writers, copywriters, short story writers, songwriters and librettists. And there are hundreds of sub-categories I could list besides these. They work in different sectors of the industry, in many cases utterly unrelated to each other and ignorant of the skills, traditions, technical requirements and career paths of each other. The world of professional writing is not really a single industry, and therefore it's unrealistic to suggest a single pathway into it. But I'll do my best in this book to point you in the right direction for the type of writer you want to be.

Top tips for preparing to be a writer

- Write with any tools you want – pen, laptop, typewriter, dictation software – but a computer file is essential when submitting work for publication.
- Typing skills will come naturally the more you write.
- Back up your work frequently and in multiple places.
- Don't give up the day job (yet!).
- Read books or watch entertainment with an active, analytical mind.
- Don't expect a life of glamour.

" *Easy reading is damn hard writing.* "

NATHANIEL HAWTHORNE

2

PRACTICALITIES
OF BEING
A WRITER

FIND THE BEST PLACE TO WRITE

'Why do writers write? Because it isn't there.'
Thomas Berger

Whenever I need to write something away from my normal writing office in my garden I sense a mild panic: will I be able to get the words flowing without my large white desk, without my Vitra mesh-backed office chair, without my dual monitors, without my exposed roof beams and without the little stains in the ceiling where the roof used to leak? It's sometimes hard to imagine writing without these comforts, luxuries and familiarities. But when that panic hits me I think of Shakespeare and all is well. Not necessarily the real Shakespeare of history, but the one brilliantly portrayed by Joseph Fiennes in the film *Shakespeare in Love*. He didn't need the latest version of Microsoft Office to create works of genius. He coped perfectly well without script layout software, without a chair, without even a pen. When a writer is in the right frame of mind it is sufficient to possess a wooden box to sit on and a feather with which to write.

The popular image of writers working in their sheds comes from authors such as Virginia Woolf and Roald Dahl who famously found that the peace and seclusion of a small studio in their garden created the optimal environment for their craft. A shed minimises disturbances and provides a sense of detachment from normal life that many writers find conducive to creativity. But the beauty of writing is that it can be done anywhere: try to be as far from a telephone and television as possible (although it's useful to have Internet access for research purposes).

Kit out your writing space with any personal items that make you feel comfortable there, like family photos and a plant or two.

Make a shelf for reference books like this one. Ensure there is space to spread out your research materials and writing, and also that there is space to put it all away tidily if you are progressing with another project simultaneously.

> **❝** *The best place to write, in my opinion, is a cafe; you don't have to make your own coffee, you don't feel that you are in solitary confinement while you work and when inspiration fails, you can walk to the next cafe while your batteries re-charge.* **❞**

J. K. ROWLING

IS IT IMPORTANT TO HAVE A SPECTACULAR VIEW WHEN YOU WRITE?

I feel a little guilty writing on this topic, because I'm about to explain why a view doesn't matter that much, and yet the vista before me as I write these words is utterly stunning. I've written parts of this book at home and abroad, and right now I'm looking at a sparkling Mediterranean Sea, gently swaying palm trees, and some awfully expensive-looking yachts all lit by an unremitting sun shining down from a cloudless sapphire sky. Has this natural beauty instilled a creative urge within me? It feels like I'm being inspired by it, and my output today has been undeniably significant. But I know from experience that my writing would have progressed similarly well had I locked myself in a windowless room. I'm nearing the end of writing the new material for this book[3], and the project has achieved a rate of momentum that makes it easy for me to keep tapping at those keys regardless of the view from my desk.

So whilst it's entirely normal, when trying to write from your kitchen table with a view of your fridge, to yearn for a sweeping panorama that floods your senses with the most wonderful and bountiful visual pleasures that our planet can provide, you have to believe that you don't need it. You really don't. Besides, many would-be writers with spectacular vistas spend far too much time staring out of the window and not enough time writing. The only thing a view is perhaps useful for is the important task of corralling your enthusiasm to the level necessary to get started on a project.

3 I didn't write this book in order, from start to finish. Non-fiction works like this can be written in any order, dipping in and out as required – more on that later.

If you've been thinking about writing a book, for instance, but have never managed to eke out sufficient thinking time from the daily grind, then take yourself away somewhere. Indulge your eyes with a view for a few hours, or take a holiday and absorb the wonder of somewhere different, fresh and invigorating. That kind of view can get you kick-started. After that you can be anywhere.

And I mean anywhere. Parts of this book were written in New York, Brazil, Spain, France and England, and on journeys in-between. Your daily dose of writing can be done wherever you can find a chair and a table – that is why your hobby (and, hopefully, profession eventually) is such a great way to spend your time. Actually, even the chair and table are optional, since sitting up in bed can be a comfortable writing position. Plus, you don't need to commute to be a writer. You don't have to share the stress of the daily rat race to and from a soulless place of work. Writers have been known to explore their creativity in places such as:

1. Any corner in their home, from a study to a kitchen table.
2. A shed or converted garage.
3. A mobile office in a camper van or large car.
4. A local library.
5. A cafe.
6. A park.
7. A beach.
8. The toilet at their place of work (one of the first authors I ever published says he wrote the first draft of his book in a cubicle during his toilet breaks at the factory where he worked, and the book eventually sold over 100,000 copies and was made into a film).
9. Commuting by train, bus or plane.
10. Using a Dictaphone whilst driving.

HOW TO FIND TIME
TO BE A WRITER

I once read a book about being a writer by an author who had some pretty odd ideas. When tackling the issue of how to find time to write if you have a full-time job, his solution was simple: get up at four in the morning and write for three or four hours before getting ready to go to work. Hmm. I think that writing (and holding down a job) requires clarity of mind. If I started getting up at four every day, I would begin to see the world through a foggy haze that would completely ruin any chances of writing anything remotely coherent. Unless, of course, I went to sleep at eight the previous evening, and that's a privilege usually reserved only for breakfast television presenters. Some habitual insomniacs and those who simply need less than the average amount of sleep might wish to argue this point.

But based on my own experience I have to begin this exploration of how to find time to write with the rule that sleep is sacrosanct. A good night's sleep is essential for the brain to be able to think clearly. Energy drinks can help in the short-term, but they are not a permanent solution to getting only twenty winks a night when forty winks is the amount recommended by medical professionals.

Given that forty winks equates to eight hours in the sack (five winks is equal to an hour's sleep, I think), that leaves sixteen hours in the day. If we accept that all great writers in history also slept for eight hours a day, then they also had sixteen hours of consciousness to work with each day. No matter how prodigious their output, no matter how great their literary talents were, none of them had more waking hours in the day than you or I. All the great novelists, poets, playwrights and copywriters (mustn't forget those ad men) had the same allocation of hours. Scientists, self-made billionaires, record-breaking sports people and professors – they all have the same hours in the day as we do.

It may appear that other writers have a body of work behind them that seems like more than one lifetime's output, but no one is born with novels under their belt. We all have to go through the slow and difficult process of learning to speak, learning to read, learning to write, and then learning to write good. I mean, write well. It's a process that normally takes up the first twenty to thirty years of our lives. So the writer's productive years begin at the same time that other things start to demand chunks of their day: the need to earn a living, the need to find a partner, and the need to bring up children. The need to keep all of those elements working in harmony seems to consume every waking minute, though. With so many daily pressures in life, how does anyone find the time to write?

The truth is that most people don't find the time to write. And yet there are many hundreds of thousands who somehow, against the odds, manage to put pen to paper or finger to keyboard. What's the secret of these people? Do they somehow stretch the fabric of time to squeeze a few extra hours in the day? No. Do they possess self-control and motivation at levels to which most people could never aspire? No. Are they all anti-social misfits who refuse to spend time with their husbands, wives, children or friends? No. Well, maybe some are, but they're in the minority.

I want to demonstrate to you that anyone – yes, anyone – can find time in their day to write. No matter what manner of maelstrom your life currently consists of, no matter how chaotic your home, no matter how pressured your job, it can be done. You can get where you want to be, from a standing start to having a literary output equivalent to at least one novel, or screenplay, or play, or whatever your chosen art, per year. You will be able to achieve this, I promise you. But it's not an instant fix. Becoming a writer requires a delicate blend of time management, psychology, charity, sympathy, understanding and cups of tea. The mind is a powerful machine, but it doesn't have a simple on-off switch. It takes time to prepare it for daily writing, to train it to accept writing as part of your routine, and ultimately to make it eager to propel your writing project forwards.

Let's start with my optimum, fantasy writing day. Forget working for a living, social life, family duties, and mowing the lawn: this is my idealistic writer's day. It's rare that I've been able to write to schedules like the following one, but the quantity and quality of what I was able to write under those conditions was fabulous. You may only ever achieve a writing day like this a few times in your life, but it's useful to look at how it works.

I structure my perfect writing day into four bursts, each two hours long, totalling eight hours:

8.00 a.m. Wake up, have breakfast, etc.
10.00 a.m. Writing
12.00 p.m. Exercise
1.00 p.m. Lunch break
2.00 p.m. Writing
4.00 p.m. Break
5.00 p.m. Writing
7.00 p.m. Leisurely evening meal
9.00 p.m. Writing
11.00 p.m. Bed

This is a day of intensive writing, usually coupled with word-count targets such as 1,000 or 1,500 words in each two-hour period. But it builds in plenty of one- and two-hour breaks to give my brain a rest. I developed this system whilst writing a book in a rented cottage in France. The cottage had no television, phone or Internet so there was nothing to stop me concentrating, and I could write between 4,000 and 6,000 words a day using this schedule. I had total support from my wife, who prepared all meals, helped with research, and would put her hand up when she wanted to speak so that I had time to finish writing a sentence or a paragraph before she interrupted. I had the rare luxury of not needing to do anything other than write, so my brain was not distracted from its important task. It's not a situation that could fairly be sustained for a lengthy period – you can't expect a partner to be a slave forever – but it was fun for a few days and it boosted the embryonic book clear of the ground.

Let's consider a more sustainable, laid-back daily schedule, such as a bestselling writer might enjoy.

9.00 a.m. Wake up
9.30 a.m. Exercise
10.30 a.m. Breakfast
11.00 a.m. Writing
1.00 p.m. Lunch break
2.00 p.m. Take a nap
3.00 p.m. Edit what you wrote this morning
5.00 p.m. Relax after a hard day's work

That's the dream. That's where we'd all like to be once our talents are recognised for what they are and our genius is loved and respected by the world. Sadly, this kind of lifestyle only comes with mega-success as a writer. The rest of us have to squeeze writing time from our already busy schedules, and it's rare to be able to find more than a couple of hours per day that we can devote to our creative passion. But hang on – there are only two hours of actual writing in the dream schedule listed above. So, in fact, all of us could write for the same amount of time per day as those lazy, cosseted full-time writers who are earning money in royalties even while they sleep. The only real difficulty lies in finding the motivation and the creative energy to use those two hours a day for writing when the temptation is to spend it snoring on the couch.

> 66 *If you want to write, you can.*
> *Fear stops most people from writing,*
> *not lack of talent, whatever that is.* 99
>
> RICHARD RHODES

WRITE EVERY DAY

Diaries make you write every day, so keep a diary. Once you're in the habit of writing every day you become a writer. Easy. Now keep going with that diary until you're ready to start your book. Write a little bit of your novel or screenplay or anything else every day. Not such a difficult transition, was it?

Let's say you want to write a novel and you manage to write one page of text on your computer a day, five days a week. That's about 500 words a day. Sounds a lot? It's only six or seven paragraphs. Hardly seems worth it when you think of it like that. But 500 words can be written in less than an hour if you're feeling inspired, and shouldn't take more than a couple of hours at worst, and at the end of the first week you'll have 2,500 words under your belt. That's easily a chapter. At the end of the first month you'll have 10,000 words. Print that out and fan through it. Feels pretty satisfying, right? Twenty pages of text printed single-spaced equates to about forty pages of printed novel. Quite a chunk of work, and something to be proud of, yet it's only taken a little part of your weekday evenings for a month.

Keep up a routine of writing for just one or two hours per working day, and well within a year you will have not only a complete first draft of a novel, but probably a couple of further drafts in the bag as well. There was no need to give up your job, get divorced or lose your social life.

A couple of hours a day could consist of your lunch break and the commute to work. Or getting up a little earlier...

Or writing during that period after supper each evening when the rest of the family is watching telly and doesn't want to speak to you anyway. It's not much of a sacrifice to make in order to get that proud feeling that you know you can write a novel in a year.

Creative writing is an arduous undertaking. Even a limerick can really take it out of you. Despite all the theories about why it's good to write something every day, it's actually very hard to write at first. Your mind will come up with dozens of things to do before the writing starts. Your washing-up will get done, your house will be cleaned and your lawn will be mowed before you run out of excuses and have to start writing. Starting is almost impossible for me. Then, little by little, it starts to flow, to gain its own momentum.

Until you experience that momentum you just have to have faith that it's going to get easier. I've known authors who can write a draft of a non-fiction book in one week. That's real, unstoppable momentum. And that's why you've got to keep struggling in those early days to push your project forward one line at a time. If you don't keep applying that effort early on, you'll never reach the point where you experience the smooth surge of creativity that can happen when words flow through your fingertips as fast as you can type them.

Reader's question:
Am I wasting my time by writing for
a couple of hours every day?

Think about the last book you read. It might have taken the author hundreds or thousands of hours to create a work for you to enjoy. Was that a waste of time? Have their words given you pleasure, made you think or smile? Imagine your emotional and intellectual experience of reading this work multiplied by all of its readers: has the author contributed in a small way to making the world a happier and better place? If you have the potential to change people's lives with your words, if only by providing them with contentment or excitement for a few short hours, is that a waste of your time? If your writing can make people better informed, better individuals and better citizens, that surely justifies your efforts. The long hours that I'm putting into writing this book never feel wasted, because I know that someone, somewhere, will be inspired to change their life and become the writer they always dreamed of being. Perhaps that person is you?

66 *The best time for planning a book
is while you're doing the dishes.* 99

AGATHA CHRISTIE

WHAT HAPPENS IN A TYPICAL WRITING SESSION?

Let's say I've managed to allocate two hours exclusively to writing. First, I need to clear my head from whatever I was doing or thinking about before. A cup of tea or a glass of wine might be the first step: the act of preparing a drink helps to flush other concerns from the forefront of the mind. A certain amount of faffing might then ensue, and by 'faffing' I'm including a brief look at Facebook, email-checking, desk-tidying, bin-emptying, chair adjustment, another peek at Facebook, perhaps a second cup of tea and a quick game of Solitaire. This might take up the first twenty or thirty minutes of the writing session, but by now I'm ready. The point is that you need not be ashamed of faffing. It may look to the untrained eye like time-wasting and procrastinating, but actually it's a vital part of the writing process that gently switches your mind from normality to the world of creativity.

Ever wondered why a tennis champion twiddles their racket and bounces the ball several times before serving? Same reason as a faffing writer: they are getting into the zone. I have another ritual to ease the transition into the zone, which is the rather mundane process of locating and opening the Word file. Take this file I'm working on at the moment, for instance. I've been writing parts of this book every day for over two months, so you might expect me to keep the document easily accessible, either on my computer's desktop or in a folder that's not buried too deep within the labyrinth of my hard disk. Actually, no. Each time I want to open this file I have to click on the following folders in turn: Documents; Stew; Writing; Books; Non Fiction; Writing Series; How to be a Writer; and, finally, New Edition. That's where

I keep this file. Once I've opened the file I immediately rename it incorporating today's date in the name, so there are dozens of clearly dated versions of this file reflecting each day's progress. Locating and renaming the file at the start of each creative session requires no brainpower, and the mindlessly repetitive nature of the task brings me into the zone.

The process of faffing may need to be repeated during the writing session, especially if you become distracted by something such as a knock at the door or a phone call. Think of it as falling asleep and entering the world of dreams. You need a certain number of minutes of relaxation in order to get to sleep, but you can be yanked from your reverie in a split second by an interruption, after which it then takes a considerable time to return to dreamland.

Getting in the right frame of mind to write is remarkably similar to forgetting the worries of the day and falling into the welcome embrace of unconsciousness.

A small number of fortuitous authors are able to skip this intermediate phase and switch instantly from the real world to the writing world, which according to my falling-asleep analogy is a kind of literary narcolepsy. I can sometimes do this myself, but it tends only to happen towards the end of a major writing project when I'm able to benefit from the momentum of the work, having settled so tightly into the groove of the writing that I don't feel part of the real world anyway.

COUNTING WORDS

How many words does a professional writer produce in a working day? In my earlier example of a bestselling author who spends two hours writing in the morning and two hours editing those words in the afternoon, they would probably move forward by about 1,000 words a day. Hardly a punishing schedule. And yet working at that pace, five days a week, is enough to produce two novels, each of 130,000 words, every year. Redrafting many times in order to get it right can halve that output, of course, but if a novelist releases one book a year it is deemed to be an extremely productive career.

That's fine for full-time novelists who are fortunate enough to know that their words will be published when completed, but for amateur authors trying to squeeze writing time into their busy lives it's another story altogether. Holding down a day job and a family and then trying to produce 1,000 more-or-less publishable words before bedtime is hugely challenging for anyone. My first novel progressed in fits and starts over many years. A typical day's contribution, when I actually managed to write anything at all, was often around 500 words. Any movement in the right direction felt good, no matter how small. I found that the word count progressed faster during dialogue scenes, and things moved much more slowly during descriptive passages.

Actually, if I average out the total words written in my novel over the period in which they were produced, it only comes to seventy-five words a day. Not exactly blistering performance. Kids write more than that in their illiterate txt msgs.

There were times when I was able to take the novel on 'holiday' with me, and this was when the word count really started to fly. I discovered that I could comfortably manage 2,000–3,000 words a day, tucked in a sunny villa with nothing else to do apart from occasional sunbathing. One week I experimented to see how far I could push the limits of my creative output. The word count nudged upwards: 4,000 a day, 5,000 a day, 6,000 a day. Then I relaxed and dropped back to 3,000 for a couple of days. Then, totally 'in the zone', I wrote a massive 7,000 words between sunrise and midnight. I know, you're thinking quality not quantity. This was all first draft stuff, of course, so literary perfection wasn't essential: getting the rough draft of the story completed was the goal. I knew I could then go back and tidy it all up. I think it's more important to finish a very rough first draft than to have a few pages of beautiful English that never become a novel because the writer's progress was so slow that they couldn't maintain their motivation.

It takes a long time to warm up enough to get the writing juices to flow so easily. You can't do it from a cold start. You have to know your story, your characters, your style and your goals for the chapter. You also have to sleep well, be in a relaxed environment, and have someone to feed and water you. You have to make sure your brain doesn't need to think about anything except writing.

The level of concentration needed to write 7,000 words in a single day was phenomenal. Other people were staying at the villa too, but I barely noticed them even though I was working on the kitchen table and they were cooking and chatting around me. At the end of the day I felt as if I was punch-drunk, my head throbbing from the marathon it had been asked to run. It was like being immersed in a virtual reality, living and breathing the story of the novel and the lives of the characters. My dreams were about the novel. My waking thoughts were about the novel. It was a great experience.

❝ *The faster you blurt, the more swiftly you write, the more honest you are.* **❞**

RAY BRADBURY

SETTING A TARGET WORD COUNT FOR EACH DAY

Provided the target is set at a realistic level then it can be a useful motivational force. The quantity of words chosen should also reflect your method of writing and the stage you have reached within the project. If your technique is slow and meticulous, not moving on until your paragraph is perfect (i.e. editing as you go), then your daily target could be as low as 300 words. If you subscribe to the fast-first-draft method, which I recommend to those embarking on hefty works for the first time due to the satisfaction and motivation to be gained from seeing a rough form take shape before your eyes, set the target high.

A top-end daily target might be 1,500 or 2,000 words. More than that is certainly achievable, but it's hard to sustain a higher rate of productivity, and to set your target higher than 2,000 words a day is likely to result in disappointment.

If you really want to achieve the maximum possible daily word count, I think the ideal conditions would be to shut yourself away in a remote hotel, full board, and alone. You'll have no distractions, no cooking or cleaning to worry about, and you will quickly be absorbed into your writing to the point where it can flood out of you at 500 words an hour. I've always considered Venice the perfect location for such self-induced literary isolation, for some reason. I've yet to try it, but I reckon four to six weeks holed up in a hotel room overlooking the Grand Canal would get me at least to the end of the first draft of a novel, if not most of the redrafts too. As I write this chapter I'm sitting at a table with a sumptuous sea view, but as I'm here with people and pets I'm lucky if I write 500 words a day. I may be halfway towards the ideal writing environment, but like most authors I can't escape the commitments of daily life which always limit my output.

Writing this edition of *How to Be a Writer* I've not set myself a daily word target, but I do have a deadline and I know from experience that as it approaches I'll automatically spend increasing hours per day working on the project, writing and rewriting, editing, deleting, rearranging the order of chapters and topics, and hopefully minimising the work of my wonderful editor to whom it will shortly be submitted.

Salvador Dali wrote his only novel, *Hidden Faces*, in four months straight, working fourteen hours a day. I don't have a precise word count for his book, but it looks like it's in the region of 150,000 words. Assuming half of the four months were spent on the first draft and the rest was devoted to redrafting, that equates to an output of about 2,500 words per day in completion of that first draft. In a fourteen-hour working day that's less than 180 words per hour. If Dali didn't spend time redrafting, preferring instead to work slowly and methodically, not moving on until each paragraph was perfect, then his pace was more likely just 90 words an hour. That's about one of his typical paragraphs. Ninety words an hour is just one and a half words a minute. Sounds incredibly slow, doesn't it? And yet to complete such a lengthy work in just four months is a rate of output to which most writers can only aspire.

Dedicating an entire day to writing, give or take a few hours for basic human functions, can be an exciting event due to its rarity for most of us. Inevitably, the foreseen potential for progress fails to materialise and a certain amount of disappointment will creep in towards the end of the day. So anticipate that and put yourself under less pressure by setting a low word-count target.

> 66 *The greatest part of a writer's time is spent in reading in order to write: a man will turn over half a library to make one book.* 99
>
> SAMUEL JOHNSON

DEALING WITH IDEAS THAT
HIT YOU MID-SENTENCE

If two ideas are fighting for control of your fingers at once – you're halfway through a beautiful description of something when a plot idea related to a different scene or chapter pops into your head, for instance – you have three options:

1. Pause your primary writing and jot down the other idea in a notebook.

2. Pause your primary writing and type your other idea into another Word file that you keep open beside or behind your main document to keep all of your notes and ideas handy. I call this second file my 'scratchpad', and it's messy and random and full of thoughts, facts and ideas. The scratchpad file can end up being thousands of words long (when it's full of character notes, plot possibilities and deleted lines that might be useful elsewhere), so I try to delete any suggestions once they get used in the main work.

3. Press 'enter' a couple of times, type your new idea quickly, then return to the passage you were working on. This is the fastest way to record your brainwaves without interrupting your work. Once you have completed the section you were writing to start with, transfer your notes at the end of your work to the scratchpad file for future usage.

KEEPING NOTES

A writer should always carry a notebook and pen (or electronic equivalent) so that when a flash of inspiration arrives, a quirky character is encountered or an intriguing snippet of dialogue is overheard it can all be kept for future reference. You can use these notes to build a library of ideas and materials that you can refer to whenever inspiration seems to evade you. File the ideas according to whether they are dialogue, character attributes, interesting words, jokes or story ideas.

❝ *A man would do very well to carry a pencil in his pocket and write down the thoughts of the moment. Those that come unsought for are commonly the most valuable...* **❞**

FRANCIS BACON

BE AN EXPERT

Decide what genre and style you want to write and read similar works. Become the best in your genre by studying it until you're an expert. Before you write your work you should be so knowledgeable about the genre that you'd feel comfortable giving evening classes on it. Achieve this by reading good and bad examples of the genre and knowing the difference. Generally the bestselling works will be the good ones, and there are plenty of bad, unpublished (and unpublishable) things to read on the Internet.

**" *Just leave your mind alone;*
your intuition knows what it wants
to write, so get out of the way. "**

RAY BRADBURY

DEVELOP A VOICE

A film director puts their stamp on a movie by their creative input (camera angles, length of scene, lighting, editing, set design, etc.) to the degree that it's possible to recognise a film by Stanley Kubrick or Quentin Tarantino or Tim Burton or Terry Gilliam from just a few frames. The way in which you as an author tackle the presentation of the creative message can make your writing equally recognisable.

You and I have read a mixture of works by other writers – some old, some recent – and that combination of reading experience is unique for each of us. Therefore, when we come to write our own works, we naturally develop a style that in some way reflects the soup of literary influences bubbling within our minds. Add to that recipe a dash of life experience and a spoonful of personality and you get to the point where your writing has a recognisable style, or 'voice'.

Is this a good thing? Should your writing stand out by having a distinctive tone? I think so. Here's why:

1. Readers develop a loyalty towards certain authors because they appreciate the word play, the pacing, the structural techniques, the wit, the descriptive colours or the sparky dialogue that these writers deliver time after time.
2. Having a personal style of writing gives you a sense of direction, a path to follow.
3. Maintaining a consistent literary voice accelerates your rate of improvement as a writer.

Not convinced? Wondering if it's better to write in a style that imitates a writer you admire who is already famous and successful? Go ahead: it's fine to develop your writing in this way. Practise emulating the style of the best writers of your genre. This sounds like copying, in a sense, but it will result in something distinctive. We're all different and inevitably when we try to write like someone else the result is a blending of literary DNA to create a new voice. Nurture this voice. It's your branding, your USP (unique selling point). Whether you achieve it naturally or by deliberately attempting to write like the best, just let your voice shout out proud and loud.

> 66 *You don't write because you want to say something, you write because you've got something to say.* 99
>
> F. Scott Fitzgerald

LANGUAGE, GRAMMAR AND PUNCTUATION

Not confident in any of these? Don't worry, proficiency in English isn't hard. Forget scary lessons at school with complicated rules that you were forced to remember without understanding why. Just remember the earlier section in this book, 'Think like a writer'. You can improve your spelling, your punctuation and your general use of the English language by reading with an active mind. Read for at least 30 minutes a day, but stay active. Observe the spelling and punctuation used by published writers. Think about the way in which their sentences are constructed. You'll be amazed how quickly you can absorb the equivalent of several years' worth of school lessons simply by reading books you enjoy and remembering to think about what you're reading.

❝ *As to the adjective,*
when in doubt, strike it out. **❞**

MARK TWAIN
THE TRAGEDY OF PUDD'NHEAD WILSON

VOCABULARY

A writer earns money from words. Words are your raw materials and words are freely available. All you need to do is pluck them out of the dictionary and arrange them in an order that will excite and enthral the reader. So it's helpful if your arrangement and selection of words is distinctive. Learn a new word each day and try to write with fresh images and words that haven't been used before. Anyone can write clichés, but only great writers can write phrases that are copied by others until they become the clichés of the future.

66 *One must be drenched in words, literally soaked with them, to have the right ones form themselves into the proper pattern at the right moment.* **99**

HART CRANE

KEEP IT INTERESTING

When you're writing it's helpful to imagine a reader who could be about to nod off or close your book at any moment. Don't let them! Keep prodding them with your prose. Surprise them. Nudge them in different places. Intrigue them. Inject some magic into every page so that they can't put it down.

Top tips on the practicalities of being a writer

- Find a suitable place to write.
- Don't worry about having an 'inspiring' view.
- Try to allocate at least two hours a day for writing.
- Get into the habit of writing every day.
- Don't feel guilty about taking the first 30 minutes of your writing session to get into the 'zone' before you actually write anything.
- Set a realistic target for your daily word count.
- Be prepared to capture your ideas whenever they strike.
- Read widely in your chosen genre.
- Develop your own writing style.
- Observe how others structure their sentences, but be original in your phrases and vocabulary.
- Don't let your reader get bored.

3

THE SECRET OF WRITING LIKE A PROFESSIONAL

THE SECRET OF WRITING LIKE A PROFESSIONAL

'I was working on the proof of one of my poems all the morning, and took out a comma. In the afternoon I put it back again.'
Oscar Wilde

At the beginning of the book I said I'd explain the difference between a professional writer and a would-be writer. It's really simple. The professional rewrites and rewrites until it's perfect; the amateur thinks their first efforts are good enough. The professional never submits a first draft because a first draft is not publishable. Even the second draft may not be publishable. Screenplays are often not taken seriously by producers until they are past the tenth draft.

At the Frankfurt Book Fair I was once approached by a writer who asked me to read a sample of her book. By page three it was obvious that this was a first draft. There were mistakes, immature-sounding phrases, excessive exclamation marks (always a sign of too much enthusiasm for a writer's own work), and a sense that what I was reading was little more than her notes. Some phrases and sentences were good enough to stay, but most needed completely rewriting. When she returned the next day I asked her whether she had given me a first draft to read. She admitted that this was the case and I had to ask her to go back and spend a year rewriting and not to resubmit until the book had progressed through many drafts. As a publisher I can recognise a first draft very easily and I won't waste my time reading beyond the first couple of pages (I only got to the third page of her book because I was waiting for someone to turn up for a meeting).

You might think this is a foolish approach – what if a future bestselling author gave me a first draft and I didn't even read it? It all comes down to economics. It's quite hard to spot a potential world-beating book if it's badly written. With my team of talented editors I know we could, in theory, take any amateurish manuscript and edit it so heavily that it emerges shiny and sparkling and ready to dazzle the literary world. But why would I put all my resources into doing so when they are better spent on books that are already written to a high standard? A team of three editors could publish dozens of books a year if they choose the best ones to begin with. If they pick badly written books, they could only publish a handful of books per year.

> ❝ *... everything in life is writable about if you have the outgoing guts to do it, and the imagination to improvise.* ❞
>
> SYLVIA PLATH

START BY WRITING RUBBISH

Keep writing, even if you think it's rubbish. It probably is, but there's nothing wrong with that. Words are infinitely malleable and even a monkey's random keystrokes can eventually evolve into a Shakespeare play given enough rewrites (by Shakespeare, not a monkey). You can only shape something into a masterpiece if you have something to shape in the first place.

Perfect poetry or prose doesn't just come out of a writer's head the first time they put pen to paper. That's a common misconception that keeps the number of professionals in the writing game relatively small compared to the millions who dream of joining them. True, there are a small number of writers who agonise for days over every syllable of every word and who are able to produce readable results in one draft, but that isn't the way the majority of successful writers work. It really doesn't matter if your daily writing output isn't very good. It's the same for all of us. The bestselling children's author Louis Sachar likens the process of writing a book to that of creating a sculpture. You create a first draft that may be completely unpublishable, but then you chip away until gradually a shape appears and you keep on chipping until you're looking at a work of art.

If you're not prepared to put in the effort to rewrite your first drafts, then the rubbish you write will remain rubbish. Not sure what a rewrite consists of? No problem, I'll take you through it.

Reader's question:
Certain parts of my book have not yet been fine-tuned, but I want to send it out to publishers anyway. Should I?

No. Redraft it and fine-tune it according to the procedures in this book before sending it out. Don't waste your time and the publisher's time by submitting something that you know to be in need of improvement. You could, however, submit the idea in the form of a short sample and a synopsis, provided the publisher is prepared to consider a partial submission (your sample must be suitably gleaming and sparkling, needless to say). Make it clear in your covering letter that the book is being redrafted and estimate the date by which it will be ready for them to see.

Reader's question:
I think books get stronger as they progress, and that is certainly true of my book; therefore, surely a publisher will want to read to the end even if my beginning is weak?

Deep breath. Stay calm. Relax. OK, now I'm ready to deal with this question without sprinkling this page with the written equivalent of an audio beep. A book that is weak at the beginning, and which the author knows to be so, is not ready for submission to a publisher. It is, by definition, in need of further drafting, and is therefore a work in progress for which an attempt at a sale should not be made. When you know part of your work needs improving, take the time and make the effort to improve it. Publishers won't read the whole book if the beginning is weak. They'll rightly cast it aside and move on to the next submission. They have plenty to choose from, after all. Most authors will have taken the trouble to improve their first chapters, and the publisher will be looking for such a work when they select the next one from the pile.

The opening pages of your work are the most important: they have to hook not only the publisher but also the reader, the reviewer and perhaps the bookseller too. Make those pages count. Write it, rewrite it, rip it up, start again, set fire to it, begin once more, edit it, tweak it, adjust it, polish it, and shine it until it's so dazzlingly brilliant that you'll need to read it through the protection of a welder's mask. Then do the same to the rest of the book. And then, and only then, can you start to think about submitting your masterpiece to a publisher.

BB *The wastebasket is a writer's best friend.* **BB**

ISAAC BASHEVIS SINGER

WHAT CONSTITUTES
A NEW DRAFT?

It's not about increasing the word count every time, unless your first draft falls seriously short of your target length. And it's not about completely starting again from scratch every time: not every word has to change. A new draft is a freshening up of the text, usually with an eye on a particular aspect of the writing. There's no need to think about everything during each draft, just focus on one thing at a time.

It's likely that less than 5 per cent of your text will change during any given draft, and yet this is usually enough of an improvement to make the writing feel as if it's starting to come to life. Ten drafts changing 5 per cent every time means that you've replaced half of what you wrote in the first draft. That's normally enough for the writing to evolve from unpublishable tripe to a gripping page-turner. Everyone's writing and rewriting will be different, of course, so I'm approximating the process. You might need to rewrite more than half of your words before you have a product worthy of being called complete. You might change very little on each draft and still end up with a polished piece.

It's not uncommon for your tenth or later draft to be bought by a publisher or production company who then wants to work with you on further rewrites. The film industry is notorious in this respect. Just as you finish your fifteenth rewrite the producer decides it would be a good idea to change it from a comedy to a thriller, and to change the sex of your lead character. Even during the shooting of the film you may be called upon to write new scenes and to change existing ones. It's the same for journalists, who have to be prepared to rewrite an article at the last minute because its tone or angle doesn't please the editor or because new facts relating to the story have emerged. The business of being a writer involves being prepared to be flexible, to accept that your work is never really finished until the book is printed or the film is in the cinemas.

A typical series of drafts for a work of fiction could be tackled as follows:

Draft 1: An approximation of the whole work

Write it quickly. Don't agonise over details of character and plot if they don't come to you immediately. Just write as it flows from inside you. Make decisions quickly and stick to them for now. For example, your two main characters are arguing. Who should win the argument? Decide on the toss of a coin if necessary (I'm not saying this is a good way to construct a story but it's better to do this than to spend so many days worrying about it and not writing that in the end you lose enthusiasm and momentum and give up). Make your choice and run with it. Don't fret about a character's name or the kind of car they drive. Don't panic if there's a hole or inconsistency in the plot.

Great chunks of this draft will subsequently be deleted, but much of it will make it through to later drafts. You can't really begin the later drafts until the first is completed so keep pushing on with this one.

A small proportion of writers say they begin the second draft shortly before the first one can be completed. This is a good idea if you're aware that you're going significantly off course and ideas are starting to come to you about a better route to take. Most writers, however, prefer to finish draft number one and feel that sense of achievement before taking a break for a few days and then reading it all through with a sense of objectivity. They make detailed notes on any problems that are apparent in that first reading, then they prepare for the second draft.

Draft 2: A tightening of the structure

This is your opportunity to think about how to fill those holes in the plot. Have you introduced something that needs to be set up earlier on? Let's say a grandmother character queuing inside a bank suddenly demonstrates pinpoint throwing abilities when a bank robber runs past with the bag of loot. She gets him clean on the back of the head with an apple from her handbag. Sounds incredible? It is. And your reader or viewer won't fall for it. But you want this scene because it's a crucial plot point. So what do you do? Easy. Go back in your story and insert a scene which shows how the grandmother came to be such an accurate shot. Perhaps she keeps chickens in her garden and shoos foxes away by throwing apples at them? You don't need to make a big play of this, just show it happening so that the reader remembers this earlier incident and therefore is able to believe in what happens in the bank.

Do you need a subplot to counterbalance the main story? Can you think of a way to weave in a subplot without adding many extra characters? Can you make the subplot relevant to the resolution of the main plot at the end?

Are there any tangential elements of your story that head off in one direction away from the action and then just come back again? Could you prune that whole sidetracking sequence without any loss to the main story? Prune away. Replace it with something that adds meaning and depth to the main plot or the subplot instead.

Does the work need to be lengthened or shortened? Professional writing is all about producing work to accepted standards and conventions. If your novel is just 40,000 words long, you'd better start finding ways to expand it to a more normal length. If your sitcom script runs to 100 pages, it won't fit the standard half-hour slot and you'd better start editing it down heavily.

The second draft is often a major rewrite if the first draft is the wrong length. A new subplot would add between 5,000 and 10,000 words to a novel or between ten and twenty pages to a screenplay. If you need more than this, you need to look carefully at the content of the main story and how it is explored. Are there enough twists to the story? Should you increase the amount of scene description? Is there enough dialogue? Do the characters get their way too easily? One effective way to add length to your writing is to increase the obstacles in the way of a character achieving their goals. Make other characters oppose them and argue against their point of view. This adds conflict and drama as well as helping you get to the desired length.

Draft 3: Development of the characters

How well do you know your characters? Can you recount their life story up to the point at which they joined the narrative? Are they believable? Are they too plastic and perfect, or do they have flaws that anyone can identify with? Would the reader care about them enough to keep reading? You need to keep accurate records of all the decisions you take about your characters' lives. Complete a character questionnaire containing enough details for you to know everything about them so that you can refer back to it every time you need to decide how a character should react to a situation.

There's a free character questionnaire available to download from my website, www.stewartferris.com.

It has been said that the essence of every story is to put a hero in a tree, throw stones at him, then bring him down again. But when he comes down he's not the same person he was before you threw those stones. By surviving the attack and learning valuable lessons about life and the toughness of the human condition your hero has changed. This change is called the character arc.

Characters need to arc during your story. They begin in one state of mind, they face challenges and grow, and they finish the story as better or wiser or different people. This is important because the reader has been rooting for them and will gain a sense of satisfaction in seeing them reach a degree of maturity as a result of their journey through the story.

All characters have wants and needs which will either be fulfilled or denied during the story. If they achieve their goals, they'll either be happier as a result, or they'll learn that this kind of fulfilment is actually empty and that other things matter more. If they fail in their quest, they'll either be affected in a depressive way or will decide that this failure has brought them some kind of symbolic success on another level. Every character who appears more than once should have an arc, no matter how small. Show it in as subtle a way as you can, but don't neglect this important facet of fiction.

Draft 4: Improving the dialogue

If you deleted all your characters' names, would it still be obvious who was talking? Probably not. So this should be your goal in this draft. Give each character a vocabulary, accent, favourite phrases and manner of speaking that gives them all complete originality. However, don't try to achieve this simply by giving everyone a different regional accent and writing it all phonetically. This would be difficult and tedious to read, and would alienate readers who are unfamiliar with those dialects.

Start by listening to how real people speak. They often have catchphrases. They may be incapable of finishing one sentence before beginning the next one. Perhaps they are always cynical in their speech, or are always trying (and failing) to be funny. Some people talk in formal tones with long words and correct grammar. Some only use the latest slang words from the street. Each person has a different agenda that taints the tone of what they say. Give colour and variety to your characters by making each individual talk in a way that is unmistakably a line from that character.

Draft 5: Working on the language and imagery

This is the time to dust off your thesaurus. Look for words that are often repeated in your text and replace them with synonyms. Closely examine the way in which you use language to see if there might be a more elegant way of phrasing some of your basic sentences. Find more interesting words, similes and metaphors than the ones you've used so far. Make sure that wherever you spot a cliché you don't rest until you've found an original replacement for it.

Read your work with an objective eye and try to appreciate whether it sounds like a mature piece of writing, or whether it's written in the same way you wrote essays and stories at school. Does your style lack confidence? Is your inexperience showing through with clumsy phrases, awkward paragraphs that don't quite make sense, non sequiturs, and shallow description? Have you neglected any of the senses in your use of adjectives to describe places and people? There's much that can be done in this draft to make your writing more polished and closer to being ready for someone else to see. But hang on a little longer – there's more work still to do.

Draft 6: Restructuring parts of the work

There are two ways to tell a story: linear and time jumping. A linear story starts at the beginning and follows events in chronological order through to the end. Time jumping is when that linear story is chopped up and the pieces arranged in a different order. You could start your novel with the big conflict from the penultimate scene, then use flashbacks to tell the story of how that conflict developed before finishing off by showing how that conflict was resolved. Or you could repeatedly jump back to snippets of a character's previous history to demonstrate how the challenge they're facing today echoes something they faced many years ago and show how the lessons learned the first time around will help to save them this time.

Would your story benefit from changing the order in which you describe the events? Perhaps starting with a more dramatic scene might help to hook the reader early on? It's not unusual for a first chapter to be very dull compared to the second chapter. The solution is easy: start with the second chapter, and either rewrite or lose the first one.

Think about the structure on the smaller scale, too. Are any of your scenes or chapters too long? Every scene should begin at the last possible moment and end as soon as possible. Anything more is superfluous to the scene. It's usually not necessary to describe the full details of your hero's car journey to the bar where he meets the heroine for the first time. What's important is the scene in the bar and the sparks that fly when these great characters interact, not the sparks that fly when he scrapes his bumper in the car park. It's for this reason that we don't normally see characters on the loo in film and fiction. It's usually irrelevant to the story. Have you noticed that people in films rarely say 'Goodbye' when ending a telephone conversation? Every line of dialogue is a precious resource that has to contribute something to the story and the character, and saying 'Goodbye' on the phone is rarely considered important enough to justify a second of expensive screen time.

Draft 7: Adding layers of conflict

I once saw a low-budget, independent film where the main character was in a crisis and needed to make a potentially controversial decision. So he went to seek advice from a friend. The friend suggested something, he thanked him and went off and did just that. I fell asleep soon after. Here was a fantastic opportunity for a scene where a passionate argument could erupt between the two characters about the choice to be made, but the writer wasn't aware that conflict is an essential part of any story. Conflict isn't just hitting or shooting people. It can exist in the angry look of an elderly spinster to her sister when the vicar flirts with her. Some of the most powerful conflicts occur when a character must make a difficult decision – cut the rope and let the other climber fall to his death, or hang on until they both fall? What makes a story interesting for a reader is the process of following the hero on his quest as he struggles against adversity at every turn. Marty McFly in *Back to the Future* didn't go back to 1955, stroll around a bit, then return to 1985 with no problems. He was in trouble from the moment he arrived, and things got more and more difficult for him. The effort to return to his own time was a titanic struggle against the odds.

Draft 8: Improving the crucial opening pages

Remember the author I mentioned earlier who showed me her book at Frankfurt and I knew after three pages that it had to be rejected? In fact, I can usually reject a book after reading a single page. Sometimes a couple of pages if I'm not too sure. Screenplays have to hook a reader by page three. If nothing has happened by page three, then that script will be discarded. Many books and scripts by new writers fail to impress the reader in those opening pages with the result that the rest of the work doesn't get read at all. Don't be depressed by this. Rejoice in the knowledge that if you can come up with just three amazing pages, you're well on the way to getting the rest of your work read.

Is there any dull description in those first pages that could be jazzed up? This is the time to recheck your earlier search for clichés and weak language. Nothing should slip through the net here because this is the only part of your work that you can guarantee will get read by the people who have the potential to make or break your writing career.

The first sentence of a novel should electrify the reader. Go to a bookshop, open up some bestsellers and read their opening words. Do any of them hook you and make you want to read on? They all should do. Spend days and days on your first sentence: it'll be worth it. John Wyndham's haunting opening to *The Day of the Triffids* captures the tone of the whole book in 21 words: 'When a day you happen to know is Wednesday starts off by sounding like Sunday, there is something seriously wrong somewhere.' And who could forget the encapsulation of an entire social structure in Jane Austen's opening words in *Pride and Prejudice*: 'It is a truth universally acknowledged, that a single man in possession of a good fortune, must be in want of a wife.'

Something should happen on the first page that symbolises the theme of the story. By the third page an event should occur that sets the story in motion and makes the reader want to keep turning the page. It's not too much to ask, is it? Read your opening pages and rewrite them if necessary. And rewrite them again. And maybe repeat the process twenty times until you end up with three pages that will make someone's day when they read them.

Draft 9: More work on the character development

You've lived with your characters for some time now. You should be able to tell whether any dialogue attributed to them really belongs to them or not. Think about whether a line truly represents how they would talk, or whether it's a remnant of your own voice which needs to be changed now that we're into the final few drafts. Check that the character arcs you set up are really believable and satisfying to the reader. Tweak them if necessary. Interconnect characters in surprising ways in order to add strands of meaning to your work.

If you haven't already done so, make one key character turn out to be the opposite of what the reader expects. This is a common plot twist technique that is usually applied in the final part of a novel or the third act of a film. Professor Snape appears to be the bad guy throughout the first two thirds of *Harry Potter and the Philosopher's Stone*, but at the end we learn that he's actually a good guy instead. The twist is surprising and exciting, because it turns on its head everything the reader thinks they know to be true, and therefore they feel anything could happen from now on.

Draft 10: Logic and consistency

Check for a logical progression of events, revelation of information, consistency in characters and their styles of speaking. This is especially important if you've made substantial changes to the plot in the previous drafts, because it's easy for details to become jumbled and forgotten. You might, for instance, have a heroine who makes a crucial call on her mobile phone towards the end of your story. During a redraft you decide to add more drama and conflict, and write a nice scene in which her handbag is stolen. This is your chance to rectify any forgotten consequences of that change and to make the subsequent necessary adjustments further down the line.

Do your characters have enough time to move between locations realistically? If the action takes place at night, have you accidentally described sunshine in the same scene? These things sound obvious and of course you know you'd never make mistakes like that, but they do happen once you start writing and rewriting, moving scenes around, changing and improving your book.

Draft 11: Proofreading for mistakes

I'm assuming you've been fixing mistakes as you spotted them on every previous draft anyway. Now take the time to look up in a dictionary any words you're unsure of. Look carefully for typing errors. Use your computer's spellcheck and grammar-check facilities, but be prepared to overrule the computer's opinions, especially with regard to its grammar suggestions. English is a rich and complex language and computers do not yet understand its subtleties.

Have one last lookout for repeated words. This isn't where the same word is typed twice in a row by mistake; it's the use of the same descriptive word twice or more on the same page or in the same paragraph. These can be hard to spot in your own writing, but it's worth weeding out as many instances as you can find and replacing them with synonyms. Recent versions of Microsoft Word make this process simple: run a search for any unusual or distinctive words in your text, and you'll see in a column every instance where that word appears elsewhere. Where appropriate you can replace, delete or rephrase the offending repetition.

Draft 12: Read the work aloud

It's amazing how many mistakes jump out at you when reading aloud, even when you think the book is already perfect. This draft can be achieved in various ways, and to gain the maximum benefit you should try them all. Firstly, invest in software that will read your work to you automatically. Not the free, robotic voices, but the more refined and accurate voices that won't make you want to strangle the loudspeakers. Close your eyes, sit back and listen to your computer as it reads back what you've written. You'll be amazed how easily you can spot missing words, repeated words and other problems that you didn't see throughout all the previous drafts simply by listening.

Secondly, print your work and read it aloud to yourself, red pen in hand. Again, errors that have survived all the previous drafts will leap out, hands up, ready to surrender to your pen.

The final method is to read the work to a sympathetic listener. Pets do not count. You might not have anyone willing to listen to a lengthy work in one go, but if you break it down to a chapter or scene per evening then you may get away with it.

Listen to their feedback, note any comments they make as well as any other mistakes that become apparent to you as you read. This should be the first feedback you receive, since it's never wise to let third parties anywhere near your writing until the first eleven drafts are complete. Digest the comments, make your own evaluation as to whether you feel they are justified, and rework the affected passages the next day if you think it wise to do so.

Additional drafts

In the original edition of this book I stopped at ten recommended drafts. In the intervening years I've discovered a couple of extra ways to improve a manuscript, which are now included above. It may seem like overkill, but this really is the minimum. In addition to all of these structured drafts you may choose also to work on some 'freestyle' drafts, where you read through the manuscript with no particular agenda, simply keeping an open mind for anything that sounds weak, wrong, insufficient, extraneous, or that you think you could do better.

> **66** *Writing is really rewriting*
> *– making the story better,*
> *clearer, truer.* **99**

ROBERT LIPSYTE

WHAT TO DO BETWEEN DRAFTS

Taking a break between drafts increases your objectivity. A day, a week, a month – the longer the better, within reason. Best not to leave it for a whole year, though, because then it's much harder to remember what you were trying to say in your writing to start with. A break of at least a month is needed to be able to read the work with truly fresh eyes, to spot its weaknesses and to be sufficiently critical to be able to make decisions about cutting poor or unnecessary text. I prefer a month between drafts, particularly if I know I'll need to cut sequences that I was really proud of when I wrote them. Somehow that month makes it marginally less painful when making those cuts, as if time has healed the wound in advance.

Don't sit idly waiting for time to pass, though. Start another project so that you don't lose the writing habit. Return to it during every break in your first project. Ultimately this second work is something to get your teeth into when the first one is ready to send off for professional consideration, and by then you'll be starting your third project in order to have something to alternate with the second.

The first draft is the hardest, and the way to ensure you get to the end of it is to live and breathe the project. Think about it when you're not writing it. Keep your project close to the forefront of your brain at all times if you want to avoid losing momentum. The moment you file the ideas away in the back of your mind for future retrieval you risk never returning to them. It's not just knowing that you have to keep writing that is important, it's thinking constantly about what you have recently written and what you will be writing that will keep you going. Be proud of your writing achievements, even if by 'achievement' we're only talking about one page, and be excited by the prospect of future triumphs. This excitement will drive you forward.

Reader's question:
Agents and publishers have told me they wouldn't sign up my novel even if I finished it, so should I give up?

It's always sensible to keep your unfinished work to yourself. In your mind you know it's going to be a great work eventually, but others will judge it as they see it: incomplete. In any case, how do you expect to hone your craft unless you write a book, rewrite it several times to get it better, then go through the same process again and again until you're capable of creating something that will excite a publisher? Feedback will always be off-putting if you show professionals unfinished work. It could take a few years before you're ready, perhaps, but don't give up. Eventually you could have a manuscript that publishers will be fighting over.

HOW TO FEEL GOOD ABOUT CUTTING THOUSANDS OF WORDS

Why can't your writing project be like a DVD of a movie, with deleted scenes and bonus features at the end? I'm sure some people would be interested to read the sequences that ended up on whatever is the writer's equivalent of a cutting-room floor. A waste-paper basket, I suppose. So keep every deleted scene or chapter or character on file. Imagine them one day forming a bonus material section that devoted readers will find on your website, and that scholars will one day study in order to try to understand your creative genius.

When you cut back your writing, the words are not gone, they have merely been moved elsewhere. Don't mourn their loss: celebrate the improved flow and pace of the main work, and anticipate the joy that your future fans will one day gain from discovering the time capsule of mini treasures.

HOW DO YOU KNOW WHEN A WRITING PROJECT IS FINISHED?

Many writers will tell you that they never finish a project: they simply abandon it. After many drafts, improving and polishing the work each time, they know there will always be something that could be enhanced if they went through it one more time. But you have to stop somewhere. You have to decide eventually that it's as good as you can realistically make it without dedicating your entire life to it at the expense of everything else.

I'll know this book is finished when I've expanded all the notes that currently litter the document (which you won't see because they'll all become chapter and sub-chapter headings in the eventual publication), when I've rearranged the topics to form some kind of logical flow of ideas[4], when I've rewritten the most awkward passages many times, when I've edited and re-edited the text, when I've slipped in some last-minute additions and changes, when I've edited it again, and then handed it in to my editor at the publishing company who will recommend a whole new set of changes, improvements and corrections.

---

4 It's not easy to place all of the sections of this book in a logical order. In trying to achieve that result I've found that most sub-chapters flow seamlessly into the next, whilst others have to be shoehorned into a space that they can only inhabit with a degree of discomfort. Some sections don't quite fit the theme of the chapter within which I've put them, and yet they are too brief to justify their own chapter. It's the job of the writer to decide on the structure of a book such as this, and to smooth over any peaks, troughs and quirks in the arrangement of its ideas and arguments so that to the reader everything feels correct, authoritative and natural.

Top tips for writing like a professional

- Amateurs write. Professionals rewrite.
- It's normal for a first draft to be unpublishable.
- If you're aware of any weakness in your writing, work at it. Don't think publishers won't notice.
- Even if you're not aware of problems with your text, wait a few days and then read it through again. Opportunities for improvement will leap out at you.
- A new draft doesn't mean changing every word.
- Focus on a different aspect of your project during each draft.
- Don't let others read your work until you've completed at least eleven of the targeted drafts listed above.
- Read aloud during your twelfth draft.
- Take time between drafts to increase your objectivity. Why not start another writing project and alternate between them?
- Don't mourn the scenes, sentences, paragraphs, characters or chapters that you decide to delete: rejoice in the improvement their absence makes to the project as a whole.

4

INSPIRATION —AND HOW TO WRITE WITHOUT IT

FINDING INSPIRATION

'Inspiration... is something one possesses by... the hard and bitter labour of every day.'
Salvador Dali

All writers need inspiration. Ideas have to come from somewhere, preferably in a way that almost knocks the writer sideways with excitement and triggers new and brilliant thoughts in a glorious chain reaction that leads to an effortless bestseller. Inspiration is useful not only for the start of your writing project, but also on a daily basis as you struggle to write each line.

So how do you position yourself so that this kind of inspiration will come to you? Is it enough just to find a writing location with a view of Krakatoa erupting? Or does inspiration come at random from within? Inspiration is when your mind makes a connection between concepts resulting in a new idea. It's often an automatic process. Songwriters have been known to wake up with an original tune in their head that subsequently becomes a number one hit for them. People sometimes dream stories or situations, which then form part of their writing. Writers claim that a change of environment inspires them. Going on holiday inspires people to write. Spending time in a culture different to your own makes you aware of details of people and life that you normally overlook.

The truth is that inspiration can come from a number of sources. If you're stuck for ideas, here are some simple ways to seek inspiration and some of the ways in which it might hit you:

1. Relax. It's hard to be inspired after a hard day at work. You need to empty your mind of the daily stresses and worries relating to your own life. Writing a substantial work requires you to live in the imaginary world you create every time you write. You have to leave the real world behind when you upload this pretend universe into your mind. That's why you need to relax in order to absorb yourself completely in your story. Inspiration will then come more easily.

2. Look into your past. Are there any unusual events in your life history that could be adapted in some way to provide you with material to write about? Traumatic events from long ago that you might find cathartic to explore in a fictional form? You may find a way to come to terms with your own past at the same time as writing a gripping narrative. Are there people you have met (and perhaps would rather have not met) that could provide the basis for the characters in your story?

3. Look around you. What do you see happening in the world outside your window? Watch the people on the bus, walking their dogs, driving past in a hurry. Imagine their lives and the reasons behind what they're doing. Are they hiding a secret? Could they be plotting a crime or planning to escape the clutches of an abusive partner? Are they spying on you while you're spying on them? The world has many layers of mystery surrounding it. Feel free to unpeel them in your imagination and place them in your writing. If you have a view that encompasses a wide area of landscape, try to imagine the details of the community that lives there, or what would happen to someone arriving there from another part of the world who struggles to cope in this alien environment.

4. Look at people you know. It's possible to draw inspiration from people you know either personally or because they're famous without libelling them. Play safe by mixing characteristics and swapping sexes. Change their age and ethnicity. What you need inspiration for is the actual personality traits not the physical aspects. Take one person's penchant for drink and another's excessive optimism and combine them with a third person's unstoppable ambition to create a new character.

5. Look at other writing. Being inspired by another writer isn't the same as infringing their copyright (although it's usually safer if there's no obvious evidence of similarity). You can create new ideas by bouncing old ones against each other. But if you want to take someone else's ideas then make sure they've been dead for at least seventy years. You could write a modern adaptation of many nineteenth-century stories without infringing copyright. You could take out-of-copyright characters and insert them into your own stories. Think also about whether other writers, living or dead, have failed to explore subjects that you think need to be tackled. Fill in the gaps that you perceive to be in the literature that's out there.

6. Look at bestsellers. Read examples of the most popular novels. Watch the top films and television shows. Go to the theatre. Listen to the radio. Choose your genre and be aware of what is successful in that genre by looking at what the modern audience responds to. Then try to think of something you could write that will also appeal to the same audience. You're building a bridge of confidence between what the public knows they like and what you want to present to them, so your writing must have elements of familiarity whilst also containing something new and stimulating.

7. Remember your dreams. Once or twice in your life you'll dream up a story in your sleep with blockbuster potential, so keep a notebook and pen by your bed just in case.

8. Look out for random thoughts. Usually they are meaningless and useless, but occasionally a flash of genius will pass unexpectedly through your head. They can strike any time, any place, so be ready.

9. Redevelop your imagination. I used the word 'redevelop' because we rarely maintain the powerful imaginative capabilities of our childhood as we reach adulthood. An adult's imagination is neglected and atrophied. Let it have the exercise it needs to become strong and useful once again.

10. Let your ideas brew. I'm a great believer in brewing. Call it percolating, gestating, procrastinating, inertia – there is something that happens in our heads when we have ideas for writing and we let them stew and bubble for days or weeks before we do anything about it. It's as if the ideas become entrenched and start to make connections in your mind. They grow like a virus, taking over your thoughts, becoming real, preparing you to start writing whenever the guilt you feel from not writing finally overpowers you.

Reader's question:
Where do the best ideas come from?

Even the oddest, weakest and daftest ideas can be made to seem excellent if well executed, so it's hard to classify a raw idea as 'the best'. But if an idea turns out to be helpful and fruitful for you, you quite rightly want to have more of them. Keep thinking about your writing throughout the day, even when you're doing something utterly unrelated, and connections will form. Thoughts will spark, triggering new ideas in a chain reaction that will provide the materials you need to complete your project. Whether it's an initial idea for a book or one of the thousands of ideas needed to complete that work, keep thinking about your writing and the ideas will come.

> **❝** *I am not at all in a humour for writing; I must write on till I am.* **❞**
>
> JANE AUSTEN

EXPLORING 'WHAT-IFS' IN YOUR WRITING

To add twists, turns and conflict to your writing, think 'What if?' For instance, what if a character is secretly connected to another character in a way that will have repercussions later? What if you change their race, age or sex? What if they have a debilitating disease? What if they despise the culture in which they live? What if someone from their past suddenly returns to their life?

History is full of what-ifs and it's the perfect place to kick-start your imagination when in need of story ideas. What if that meteorite hadn't killed off the dinosaurs? We probably wouldn't have had a human history to start with. What if the Roman Empire had lasted a thousand more years than it did? What if Hitler had never started the war? Most of those post-war baby boom kids wouldn't have been born, so my parents might not have existed and therefore nor would I. It's quite disturbing to think that I might owe my existence to the mad decisions of one of the most evil men in history. And I'm not the only one – millions of people are alive today who wouldn't have been born without that war taking place. Equally, millions of people have never had the chance to be born for the same reason.

There are many chance events in history: things happened, other things nearly happened which would have led to other things but didn't, and so on. What if Charles Babbage had not argued with the man he was employing to construct his Difference Engine so that the thing had actually been built? The world came within a hair's breadth of having computing power almost a century earlier than its eventual arrival. Think about it: a powerful, logical, mathematical computer could have been introduced in the Victorian age. Electricity was already in use by then, so the mechanical machine might have become an electronic computer very quickly.

Was electricity in use far earlier than we think? There are objects in museums, dating from thousands of years ago, that appear to be electroplated. There is an ancient 'battery' discovered in Baghdad, close to where the electroplated items were found. What if that brief spark of electrical usage hadn't died out for two thousand years, but had developed steadily, as it did starting from its 'rediscovery' in the seventeenth century? Could Galileo have been an astronaut instead of an astronomer? Could Chaucer have been a screenwriter instead of a poet? All these things were possible. Humans stopped evolving tens or even hundreds of thousands of years ago. The raw material brain power to do everything we do today has been around since before the Ice Age. We are fortunate to live at the culmination of a few hundred years of progress in science, medicine, technology and philosophy. It hasn't been steady progress, but the result of all the random and crazy things that have happened in known history is the world we live in today. Twist any one of those events and you have the genesis of an original story.

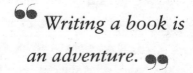

**" *Writing a book is*
an adventure. "**

WINSTON CHURCHILL

95

THE SECRETS OF WRITING WITHOUT INSPIRATION

*'Inspiration is wonderful when it happens, but
the writer must develop an approach for the rest
of the time... the wait is simply too long.'*
Leonard Bernstein

Imagine a machine that could write fiction for you. All you need to do is make a cup of tea, sit at your desk, switch on the machine and watch in awe as original prose starts to flow in front of your eyes. Sentences begin linking together to form paragraphs, and, over time, the machine continues to perform the magical evolution of paragraphs into chapters, and chapters into books.

The magnificent machine I have just described is real. And there's no need to rush out to the shops looking for it because you already have one of your own. The machine is your own mind. A writer's brain is an astonishing piece of equipment, capable of infinite literary miracles, sometimes able to create, out of nothing, works that are more valuable than gold.

That's the theory, but things are usually not so easy. Turning a blank screen into words that others will want to read – and might even want to pay to read – is an uphill struggle. We wait for inspiration and all too often we find that inspiration doesn't come. So can we write without it? When I began to explore this question in my eBook, *How to Get Inspired to Write*, I realised that there was an abundance of methods we writers could master to encourage more frequent visits from Auntie Inspiration, but equally I discovered that the secret to writing professionally and consistently is to learn the tricks of writing without inspiration.

What does writing without inspiration actually mean? It's simply the opposite of the creative genius tearing out tufts of hair in an agony of indecision and frustration whilst waiting for their muse to descend. It means getting on with your writing no matter what. It's business-like. It's efficient. It gets the job done with no fuss, no theatrics. It makes life bearable for the writer's family and it makes writing an unfailingly pleasurable and satisfying experience.

Some authors enjoy waiting for those rare moments when ideas flood their senses, causing words to gush forth from their fingertips. But if they write nothing between one inspirational event and the next it could take them a decade to complete a single book. You can't write professionally on that basis. Apart from the obvious inability to meet deadlines, it's difficult to improve as a writer if your creative sessions are separated by weeks or months.

The goal of writing without inspiration is to be able to write to a high standard regularly. You should be able to sit at your desk and work almost as easily as if you were chatting on the phone. You don't need to wait to feel inspired before calling up a friend for a natter. It's a structured routine: you tell them it's you calling; you ask how they are; they ask how you are; you tell them what you've been up to; you pretend to be interested in what they've been doing; you make fun of mutual friends and briefly comment on the celebrity twaddle or politics you read in the papers. Finally, you talk about when you'll next get together and you say goodbye and hang up. It's easy. You're probably unaware that a casual conversation follows a structure, but when you analyse it there are clear turning points that arise each time.

The same is true of literature. Many aspects of creative writing can be carried out in a structured, organised manner. When you follow these routines you're able to eliminate the need to wait for inspiration. In many ways it's almost as simple as the writer's equivalent of painting by numbers, but don't let that put you off. It doesn't mean that your writing needs to be dumbed down or amateurish. On the contrary, following these structures frees you up to concentrate on the quality of your writing rather than spending all your time hunting for ideas about character or story.

Creating characters without inspiration

Let's start with characters. Struggling to come up with original and fresh-sounding names? Use a dictionary of baby names, or take a peek at my little eBook *Unusual Character Names for Writers*.

Why have 'Sarah' when you could have 'Seraphina'? Why have 'Mark' when you could have 'Marmaduke'? Most books of baby names also give the origin and meaning of the names, and it's fun to choose a name that fits (or which is the opposite to) the character.

The next step is to decide on the details of the people whose fictional lives are in your hands. On my website there's a free questionnaire that you can download and use to fill in all the aspects of every character. It's all there, from their political views to their qualifications, from their flaws to their star sign, and it makes the task of creating fully rounded characters much easier. I keep my character questionnaire handy when I'm writing so that I don't forget the idiosyncrasies and foibles of each person – otherwise inconsistencies can sneak in unnoticed. Answering preset questions is simple compared to waiting for inspiration when trying to think up a new character. There is also a section in which you can assign a unique vocabulary of key words to them (how someone says hello, for example, can portray a great deal about their personality: using 'wotcha' as a greeting, or 'hi', 'yo', 'wassup' or 'howdy' suggests someone entirely different from 'good morning').

Creating a plot without inspiration

There are two excellent tricks that can eliminate the need for inspiration when creating a plot. The first method is to copy a storyline from someone else. Take a moment to recover from the shock and anger you're feeling at this suggestion. Surely no decent, self-respecting writer would copy a story from another author? Could anyone do such a thing and keep their reputation intact? Actually, yes. Shakespeare's reputation is pretty solid, despite taking the plots for his plays from other writers. Of course, I need to qualify this point with a reference to copyright laws. Generally, the essence of any story cannot be copyrighted. Copyright refers to the detail and the language used, but a plot in its distilled, purest form is available to anyone. When you break any story down to its components – Girl meets and falls for Boy 1,

Girl meets and dislikes Boy 2, Boy 1 tells her Boy 2 is a bad person, Boy 1 and Boy 2 fight, Girl hates Boy 2 even more, Girl discovers Boy 1 lied about Boy 2, Girl falls for Boy 2 – you have the building blocks with which to construct your own story. The plot summarised above was the basis for a bestselling book and film, *Bridget Jones's Diary*, but that book was itself based on the essence of the plot of *Pride and Prejudice*. It is a fortunate peculiarity of the written media that plotlines with a recognisable heritage are not considered as cheating, but are often applauded as works of genius.

The second trick for building a plot without waiting for a flash of inspiration is to use the Hollywood story structure. Again, this revelation often appals writers with lofty literary ambitions, but the three-act structure to which 99 per cent of Hollywood movies adhere is a device that can be traced back to Greek tragedies written thousands of years ago. My own studies of Hollywood story structure are summarised in a chart which can be downloaded for free from my website. It contains fifteen markers that you can follow to ensure a gripping, entertaining story.

A professional novelist friend of mine starts creating her books with a spreadsheet into which the plot points of the Hollywood structure are entered in columns, together with the number of words that each section should contain. So, let's imagine you're writing a novel with a target word count of 100,000. If you want to follow the Hollywood formula for its plot, the first major turning point in the story (in which the hero's initial plans are turned upside down and they embark on a new challenge) comes at about page twenty-nine of a 120-page screenplay. That's close enough to a quarter of the way through, which equates to 25,000 words. So you know that roughly around the 25,000-word mark you need to insert this turning point in the plot. There are many other points in the story which can also be pinpointed in this way.

By threading your characters through these predetermined plot twists and turns, you don't have to worry about inspiration and you can be confident that your story will satisfy your readers. The structure has worked for millennia, and it can work for you, too.

If you don't have a clue what this means, just watch any Hollywood film and see what happens about half an hour into it (one page of script is normally the same as a minute of screen time). Take *Apollo 13*, for instance: half an hour into the film is when the spaceship explodes and the characters are no longer planning to land on the moon – they are now working out how to get home alive. That's a perfect example of the first turning point in the plot. Download my movie structure and follow any film with a stopwatch, noting when the generic points in my summary happen on screen. If you create a story that follows a tried and tested structure, you can free your imagination to focus on dialogue, language and imagery.

Successful writing is about momentum. Get into the habit of writing every day and you'll build momentum into your work, and once that happens, you'll find that inspiration plays less of a role in helping you to keep moving. Your brilliant mind will get into the routine of doing what you want it to do, and if you also exploit the secrets of writing without inspiration then you are on the fast track to success.

Reader's question:
What if I run out of ideas once I've started a major writing project?

Happily, this tends not to be the case for most authors. The very act of embarking upon a major project such as a novel or stage play triggers a cascade of ideas. They don't come at once, and they always start slowly, but by getting into the writing habit and pushing forward with the project a little each day, the first trickle of ideas will soon spark a concatenation of useful and ingenious thoughts, connections, characters and situations that will propel your project towards its conclusion.

Top tips to find inspiration and to keep writing without it:

- Relax.
- Take ideas from your past experiences.
- Write about the places and people around you.
- Read.
- Write down dreams and random thoughts.
- Constantly thinking about your writing will trigger new ideas.
- Take a moment in history and give it a twist, e.g. what if John F. Kennedy's assassin had missed?
- Use a dictionary of baby names to get fabulous names for your characters.
- Use the free questionnaire from www.stewartferris.com to take the pain out of creating fully developed characters.
- Take a classic plot and rework it into your fiction.
- Don't be ashamed to follow a Hollywood plot structure.

WRITER'S BLOCK

The mental block that brings our creativity to a seemingly immovable halt is an unavoidable aspect of our trade. But don't think it's a disaster when it hits you: think of it as a perfectly natural part of the writing process, an extension of the procrastination and faffing with which each writing session begins.

Once you've lost your fear of writer's block you can now think about how to get past it, and the best way past it is simply to write. Write about why you feel you can't write. Write about your frustration at feeling uninspired. Write about why it's so unfair that everyone else seems so easily to be able to get their creative juices flowing freely while the movement of your juices is more akin to that of a glacier.

Write about what you had for breakfast. Write about what you wished you'd had for breakfast if you hadn't run out of eggs and sausages. Write about how you'll be glad you didn't have a fry-up today when you next step on those bathroom scales. Before you know it, you've been writing hundreds of words and the idea that you're suffering from writer's block suddenly seems ridiculous.

The words you've written so far were of no use to your main project, obviously, but the little exercise has helped to get your mind closer to the zone in which it will be able to contribute something of value.

I've listed many more ideas for getting past a state of literary inertia at the end of this chapter.

" *If you get stuck, get away from your desk... whatever you do, don't just sit there scowling at the problem.* "

HILARY MANTEL

HOW NOT TO GIVE UP

All the creative advice in the world is of no use to you if you can't find the motivation to continue. Major writing projects are marathon slogs, and getting to the finish line requires more determination than most people naturally possess. Here are my three top tips for staying motivated while you write:

1. Monitor your word count or page count. Celebrate every milestone.
2. Each evening, print out what you wrote that day. Admire how the words look on the page. The papers also serve as a backup in case something happens to your digital files.
3. Add today's printouts to the rest of your work from previous days and hold them in your palms. Appreciate the weight of what you've written: words on a screen have no mass, so it's helpful to connect to the reality of your achievement and to feel it in your fingertips.

Top tips to beat writer's block

- Write about how the weather is doing and what your plans are for the weekend and how you feel about the state of the economy and why you can't write and you'll realise you've just written a page.
- Get some air and clear your head. So many ideas come to writers when they stop trying to have ideas, so go for a walk and see what happens.
- If you don't want to go outside, visit the smallest room in the house. It's where most of my ideas seem to find me.

- Stop thinking, just write from the heart. Feel the passion and the pain of your characters and let it flow through your fingers.
- Go to a different part of your work and write from there. You don't have to write in a linear fashion.
- Read another writer's work. It makes sense to timetable some reading sessions into your day to stop your creativity running dry.
- Forget writing well – just write badly until you get through this patch, then come back and improve it later.
- Read what you have already written – this will get you back into the flow by uploading it to the front of your mind and will establish enough momentum for you to push the work forwards.
- Set a time limit in which you will write just one page and force yourself to go for it.
- Make a list of ways in which your work can be improved, then tackle one subject from that list.
- Think of a sparky new character with a tangential agenda to the main action that will throw everyone off course if introduced right now.
- Come at the scene from another perspective, such as from the point of view of a different character.
- Take a nap. Sleeping on a problem enables the mind to work it through, and occasionally rewards you with a solution when you wake up.
- Make a list of every direction in which this scene could potentially go. Delete the ones you're not happy with and start writing the winning idea.

- Throw a googly at your characters. Give them an unexpected problem to deal with and write their way out of the dilemma.
- Start writing another project, and when you get stuck for ideas just return to the original one.

66 *Being a writer is a very peculiar sort of a job: it's always you versus a blank sheet of paper (or a blank screen) and quite often the blank piece of paper wins.* **99**

NEIL GAIMAN

5

BOOST YOUR CREATIVITY WITH TECHNOLOGICAL WIZARDRY

*'Getting information off the internet is like
taking a drink from a fire hydrant.'*
Mitchell Kapor

We all want to leave as significant an impact in the world of words as did the great writers who went before us, and we have so many advantages that they could never have dreamed of. We can write on our phones, on our tablets, our laptops, our desktops and, even, on pieces of paper. We have software to guide us, correct us, inspire us, remind us and encourage us. We have access to all the world's history, science, religion, stories and biographies at our fingertips. We have machines and technology to make our daily lives easier – washing machines, cars, plumbing, electric lights, central heating. Could John Milton save time by heating his room at the flick of a switch? Did Geoffrey Chaucer have the option of writing after dark without straining his eyes by dim candlelight? Could Arthur Conan Doyle find information in seconds without leaving his desk? Life is far easier for us on so many levels. This chapter of the book looks at some of the ways in which writers can use technology to their advantage.

> 66 *Lock up your libraries if you like, but there is no gate, no lock, no bolt that you can set upon the freedom of my mind.* 99

VIRGINIA WOOLF, *A ROOM OF ONE'S OWN*

USING WRITING SOFTWARE FOR PLOTTING AND STORYBOARDING

Traditionally, stories have been worked out by writers using pieces of paper, perhaps writing a summary of each scene on a postcard and sticking them to a wall so that the progression of the main plot and its relation to the subplots can be seen clearly, making it easy to change the order of events and add or subtract characters and storylines. Various brands of software have been created in order simply to replicate this process. Don't be afraid of storyboarding software, because in essence that's all it does. Use it to tidy your workspace and to give you the flexibility to continue working out your story from different locations without bringing all those little cards and bits of paper with you. But, inevitably, software can be far more powerful and useful than simply emulating the arrangement of pieces of paper.

These programs can help with structure, subplots, twists, turning points, character arcs and notes. They can make suggestions, point out problems, and help you to navigate the complex journey from the beginning to the end of your story.

USING WRITING SOFTWARE FOR LAYOUT AND TECHNICAL FORMATTING

For writers of novels, poems and short stories, a simple word processor is all you need because the layout requirements for your genres are straightforward. Most publishers want text delivered in a plain font, size 12, with double-spaced lines and wide margins. The spacing gives them room to scribble their notes and corrections onto your manuscript. Check each publisher's website before submitting to make sure you comply with their requirements.

Writers of scripts, however, have more complicated layouts to which their works must adhere, and that's why software has been developed to simplify this process. For example, television scripts are laid out in two halves. The right-hand side of the page is where your script goes, the left-hand side is for the camera script, which you can leave blank. But film scripts are centred and some elements of them cover the full width of the page.

There are free templates available which do all of the complex formatting in Word for you, and there are stand-alone programs that contain their own word-processing capability in addition to layout tools and helpful gizmos to speed the writing process. Professional scriptwriters tend to use layout software that is designed to make formatting so simple that all they need to do is concentrate on their writing, not on tabs, font size, spaces, capitalisation and all the other intricacies involved in a page of script. I've put some links to free templates on my website: www.stewartferris.com. There are also links to software most commonly used by professional writers.

IMPROVING DESCRIPTIVE REALISM WITH GOOGLE STREET VIEW

Tintin's author, Hergé, rarely visited the places he drew and wrote about, relying instead on photographs of the locations where he set the action. In the 1930s, using other people's photographic reconnaissance probably seemed like a modern technological shortcut for a writer. In the twenty-first century, a new research tool for writers has arrived, one that Hergé could never have envisaged in his day. It's called Google Street View. I've managed to visit many of the locations mentioned in my fiction, but there are a few that I haven't got around to seeing yet. The early drafts of these locations were based either on guidebooks or on my imagination. With Google Street View I now have the ability to drop from the sky onto the street, look at the building I want to write about, explore the surrounding streets, see the direction of the traffic, the angle of the sunlight, the detail of construction materials, window styles and even wall plaques. It's not quite as good as being there in person, but it's quick, free, and a step up from what Hergé was able to do.

PORTABILITY OF COMPUTING EQUIPMENT

Benefit from the freedom that we writers are so fortunate to possess by investing in a laptop or tablet that's small enough to take your project anywhere. We're the first generation to have this luxury, so make the most of it. Be creative in a library, a cafe, a bus, a beach, a park or a boat. I can (just about) remember buying a compact typewriter to take on holiday with me so that I could write in the south of France one summer, and that heavy and noisy machine was not anywhere near as useful as having a fully featured word processor in my pocket. My recollection of the time of tangled typewriter ribbons and jammed keys makes me truly appreciate the affordability and portability of computers today.

" *This is how you do it: you sit down at the keyboard and you put one word after another until it's done. It's that easy, and that hard.* "

NEIL GAIMAN

INSTANT ACCESS TO
A DICTIONARY AND A
THESAURUS FROM WITHIN
A WORD PROCESSOR

Whenever I received emailed book submissions I would open them in my copy of Word, and then stare in horror if my software displayed a sprinkling of red underlining indicating spelling errors. Sometimes the red lines are there because the writer has used foreign words or names not in the dictionary, which is fair enough, but if there are ordinary English words misspelled and underlined, that is inexcusable. A simple right-click will reveal the computer's suggested replacements. It's as if the dictionary comes to you and opens itself on the appropriate page and hands you the word you need. It really couldn't be easier than that.

Obviously, you have to apply some common sense because sometimes the software guesses your intended word incorrectly, sometimes it applies the underlining incorrectly (especially if you're writing in American English with the British English dictionary turned on and vice versa) and needs to be ignored, and sometimes you're being creative in your use of language and want to invent a new name, word or hybrid that the computer doesn't recognise.

We all make typing errors, and many of us also don't know how to spell every word we want to write, so use the help that is available at your fingertips. I recommend the following procedure:

1.   Don't worry about spelling mistakes whilst working on your first draft.

2. Look for words underlined in red when you come to the proofreading draft.

3. Select the correct word from the drop-down menu provided by the software.

4. If there is no suitable suggestion, retype your word with a different spelling and try again. Sometimes complicated misspelled words are not recognised by the software until you get a little closer to the correct arrangement of letters.

5. If you're sure that your word is correct and is simply missing from the software's dictionary, or if it's a name, right-click and 'add to dictionary'. This will prevent future instances of the word from cluttering up the page with red marks, and will make it easier to spot genuine mistakes. I do this with any character and place names to which the dictionary objects.

6. If the computer thinks you've made a grammatical error, it may underline a word or phrase in green. This will need to be resolved (usually by clicking 'ignore once', since grammar suggestions are rarely as useful as spelling suggestions) before you can fix any spelling issues in the same line.

The thesaurus tool is even easier to use. When you find yourself in need of a wider vocabulary, perhaps to avoid using the same descriptive word twice in a paragraph, just right-click on the word you'd like to replace and choose 'synonyms'. A small number of suggested substitutes will appear, and by clicking on one of them you have made your replacement. If you're not convinced that the new word is appropriate in the context in which it appears, right-click on the new word and choose 'look up': provided you have an Internet connection you'll get a selection of online definitions and examples of usage for the word.

USING FREE RESEARCH RESOURCES AT PROJECT GUTENBERG

Project Gutenberg is an Internet marvel for modern writers. With thousands of out-of-copyright books digitised and available free of charge to download as eBooks, it provides access to searchable reference works and literature that would bury our homes if we possessed them all in printed form. Just search online for 'Project Gutenberg' to find this information. I regularly use a downloaded thesaurus from Gutenberg and keep it open in a window adjacent to my writing project, so that if the thesaurus suggestions within Word are insufficient I can click 'find' in the thesaurus, copy and paste the word to the search box, and instantly see a vast range of suggestions, the more exotic of which I can then cross-check by right-clicking and selecting 'look up'. Downloaded reference works like this can work seamlessly with your writing files. Large or multiple computer monitors are useful when working in this way.

RESEARCHING FACTS ONLINE

Wikipedia may not be 100 per cent authoritative, but it's usually a reasonable starting point for researching facts for your writing. I use it whenever I need to include details of history, medicine, geography, politics, technology – anything of which I'm not absolutely certain gets checked on that site, and then cross-referenced on independent websites to make sure the information is correct. The process is fast and efficient, and that's essential when I might need to look up dozens of facts during one writing session.

" Put it to them briefly so they will read it, clearly so they will appreciate it, picturesquely so they will remember it, and above all, accurately so they will be guided by its light. "

JOSEPH PULITZER

RESEARCHING THE COMMERCIAL VIABILITY OF YOUR PROJECT BEFORE YOU START

There's nothing wrong with writing what you want to write regardless of the likelihood of finding a buyer for it, if that's what you want to do. It's also perfectly legitimate to write with the intention of self-publishing from the outset, or just to write for the pleasure of it. But if your goal is to write something that might be produced or published by a third party then this exercise could be a valuable one.

It's more of an art than a science, with the aim being to ascertain via the Internet whether your idea for a creative work has a realistic chance of being sold when complete. The result of this research might convince you to carry on, or it might encourage you to tweak your concept or even to change it fundamentally.

It's an imprecise process because any type of writing in any format or genre could, in theory, find its market, so we're only dealing with broad generalisations and statistics.

Feel free to buck any trend and prove everyone wrong.

So how can you assess the commercial viability of an idea?

1. Establish the broad genre in which you intend to write (novel, play, film, poem, etc.).

2. Within that broad genre, identify the specific genre of your project (comedy, romance, horror, thriller, etc.).

3. Run an Internet search with wording along the lines of 'the market for...' inserting your genre of writing project into that phrase. I just ran a search for 'the market for romance novels', and found reassuring results – one site reports that 'romance novels are big business'. That's an encouraging start. If I was planning to begin work on such a novel, I would then study the bestseller charts to find which subgenre of romance was the most popular. At the time of writing there's a craze for erotic romantic fiction, which currently dominates the romance charts, so I would seriously consider whether I could write in the subgenre since it's obviously in high demand. A similar search for the market for plays resulted in dozens of specific theatres and venues asking for submissions, as well as competition opportunities and other advice for playwrights. But many of these submission requests were for short works, and so if I was intending to write a new play I would consider writing something that fulfilled the current specific requirements of producers wanting short works rather than full-length scripts.

4. If you want to write a book, use the Amazon rankings and bestseller charts to get an indication of the likely level of interest for what you intend to write by looking at the sales rankings of similar books. If your kind of book dominates the charts then there is clearly an appetite amongst readers for what you have to offer. But remember that there are many sub-listings on the website, and a title's popularity

can vary depending on which ranking you use: a book on rowing, for instance, can be listed at a sales ranking of over 200,000 on Amazon overall (an apparently unimpressive showing), but simultaneously it can be in the top ten in Amazon's more specialist sub-charts such as Books > Sports, Hobbies & Games > Water Sports > Boating > Rowing. To write something that tops its subgenre chart is an impressive achievement, although the higher the number of categories through which you have to navigate to get there, the lower the number of sales needed to make an impact. It's impossible to give specific sales figures in relation to chart positions because they vary hourly, but there are some sub-categories that can be dominated with only a trickle of sales each day.

5. Read reviews from readers and critics of works that are comparable to yours, and imagine how they would respond to your writing. Are you heading in a direction that could potentially result in favourable reviews? Have you taken on board any specific criticisms of the work of your rivals?

6. If you're writing a script, are television, radio and film companies currently making the type of programme or film you want to write? Are you hindering your chances by using too many cast members and sets? Search online for requests for scripts to see if they specify any restrictions. Many low-budget film producers, for example, seek screenplays that use five or fewer locations. Some even ask for just one or two locations. By writing something within these limitations you will increase the potential market for your work.

BLOGGING

What is a blog?

It's short for 'weblog', which in turn kind of means it's an online diary. But it's actually much more than that, and for any writer it's a useful and versatile tool as well as a lifestyle choice and a showcase for your talents.

Why should you set up a blog?

Because it's free, it's quick, and for the following career-related reasons:

1. It gets you in the writing habit.
2. It establishes you 'on the map' as a current writer.
3. It gives you a platform to talk about anything you like, although I'd recommend you mainly talk about your literary efforts.
4. In addition to blogging about yourself, you can review books, films, television shows and other blogs, and you can comment on current affairs – especially those which are relevant to your genre of writing.
5. You can post samples of your writing and choose whether readers can comment on them.
6. You can develop a following of readers and let them know about your progress as you write your magnum opus.

Who will read it?

As soon as you post a blog entry it's simple to post a link to it on Facebook, LinkedIn, Twitter and any other networking sites you care to frequent. This doesn't guarantee readership, but it at least makes your contacts and connections and followers aware of it. The best thing that can result from this is that one or more of them will post a link to your blog to all of their contacts, and perhaps some of those contacts will do likewise, and so on. That is how things go 'viral'. When it happens, it happens faster than you can blink.

> With a blog of the right tone and content for your captive audience there's always a chance that your post will achieve escape velocity and shoot out far beyond those people in close orbit around you.

How much should you write?

Anything from a paragraph to a couple of pages is usually adequate. I aim for about 400–600 words, which is adequate to explore a topic in brief. Write whatever feels comfortable, and don't fret over it to the detriment of your main writing project. Blogging about your day, your achievements or your thoughts on something that happened in the news should only take an hour at most. There's no need to go through my twelve-draft process – just make sure you give it a quick proofread before uploading it.

How often should you blog?

I tried to blog daily for a period of three months. In reality, I managed about twenty posts a month. It's fine to blog whenever you like, but if you want to build up a following of readers then the more often you do it the better.

Example blog posts

The following blog samples are genuine postings that I uploaded whilst editing and redrafting a novel. Although the blogs are about specific challenges I faced with that novel, I think the subjects they deal with are of sufficient interest to any writer.

Sample blog: Celebrating the completion of the latest draft of the novel

Today I completed the latest draft of my novel. Phew. Decided to celebrate with a ride along a deserted south Atlantic beach on a rented bicycle followed by a pizza and a can of Coke. We novelists know how to have a good time. This draft was started at the beginning of March, so it's taken me almost three months to complete. That's nothing in the grand scheme of this book, which I started way back in the last century, and which received practically no attention from me at all between completing the first draft in 2001 and waiting until I had the necessary time this year to devote to the task of completing the rewrites.

For this draft I've gone through the entire novel, sometimes making changes to details of punctuation and word order, sometimes rewriting extensively, and sometimes adding entire pages of new text where I felt it was needed. I didn't have a specific agenda for this draft: I felt it was important just to familiarise myself again with the story as well as fixing and improving the writing along the way. Sections have been cut and sections have been added, but what started out as 167,000 words is now 174,000 words.

In the final few days of this edit I needed to update a few things. For example, in one scene the hero, Matt, is flown by the US Air Force in an F14 fighter jet in my original draft, penned late last century. Turns out that the F14 was retired from service in 2006. Rewriting this sequence required almost a whole day researching the type of plane that replaced it, together with its fuel capacity and range, its in-flight refuelling techniques, its weapons and defensive systems, its ejector seat system and the survival rations a pilot would have if he had to bail out. Readers can be very fussy if they discover any details like those are inaccurate.

There was also a section that I had already updated twice before in previous drafts to bring it up to date, but which now seemed antiquated once again. Originally the Guatemalan scientist characters were storing important information on floppy disks. I updated this in the late nineties to writeable CDs, and then in 2001 to writeable DVDs. But people don't really do that these days – it's currently either USB flash drives or USB external drives, so I had to change it again. In the future most storage will probably be online, but that doesn't make for great drama: I have special forces soldiers fighting their way into a research compound to steal data, and it wouldn't be as exciting if they just sat in an Internet cafe and downloaded it.

The scrolls referred to in the title of the book appear towards the end of the story. I've written each of the scrolls in full, and they tell the story of the rise and fall of an ancient civilisation and the terrible thing they have set in motion that threatens our world today. The description of the actual discovery of the scrolls was rather skimpy in the original draft. Maybe I was writing quickly, knowing I was close to finishing the first draft after writing it for several years, keen just to get it finished? It needed more dramatic tension, more detail, more realism. So I've spent this week researching the Dead Sea Scrolls: what they were made of; why they survived for two thousand years; how they were handled; how they were scanned. Now when the archaeologists see the scrolls for the first time the detail and accuracy make the scene so much more gripping.

I also researched whether ancient scrolls could be read without unrolling them – turns out there's a machine in England the size of a small village that can read rolled-up text using ultra-powerful X-rays. But this won't be available to my characters in Cairo so I had to develop an alternative system for them to use to open and scan the ancient texts without inflicting too much damage.

So what's next? I wanted to have this novel completed by the end of May, which would have required at least three or four drafts to have been written by about now. Those subsequent drafts won't take as long as this one, but I do have some fairly complex subplots to weave in and I think I need to extend my three-month schedule by an extra month. So 30th of June is now my deadline for finishing the book. I'll keep on blogging about my progress as much as I can during that time, and I'll also remind myself of the big celebration that awaits this novel's completion: a really big pizza and two cans of Coke.

Then it's time to start thinking about the sequel, and I've already got ideas for that. One of the ideas is to write the book in 6 solid months instead of spread over 14 years, which I think is the best idea for a book I've ever had.

Sample blog: A new novel is born

A weird literary phenomenon happened yesterday. I got up fairly early to start work, about 7 a.m., but 'Er Indoors was sound asleep – as was Pooch on the end of the bed – so I left them in their slumber. Ordinarily I would go back an hour or so later, armed with a cup of coffee, to begin the slow process of bringing her back to consciousness. Only I didn't. I left it until nearly 10 a.m. before putting the coffee next to the bed. Still she didn't wake up, so I crept out and left her there. The day before she had been working incredibly hard restoring our house and I knew she needed to rest.

So there I was in my converted garage, tapping away on my computer and making hardly any progress at all on my novel, when at about 10:15 Katia showed up, barely awake, telling me she had just downloaded a future bestselling novel from the cosmos in her sleep. She knew the story in great detail and had even witnessed scenes from its movie adaptation. Apparently Einstein used this trick – he didn't actually think up boffy stuff himself, he just downloaded it into his subconscious from the cosmic eBook library in the sky.

I've experienced useful and creative dreams too. When I was eleven years old I bought a bottle holder to put on my bicycle, but despite a whole day trying to fit it I couldn't attach the components to the frame of the bike. I went to sleep frustrated, but in my dream I solved the problem – the flat metal brackets needed to be bent backwards around the frame. In the morning I tried it out, and it was a perfect fit. More recently I've had dreams about movie plots which seemed totally logical and exciting whilst I was asleep, but the moment I woke up I would realise that the story was insane and full of holes.

Katia's story, unlike my own dreams, was completely coherent from start to finish. It was also interesting and original, and not entirely unrelated to some of the themes in *The Sphinx Scrolls*. Probably wouldn't be a sequel, but it could be an equal. She was convinced it was a bestseller because that was how it appeared in the dream. So I put my own writing to one side and opened a new Word document called 'Katia's Story' and wrote down everything she told me. I then added details of my own which I thought would enhance the story, and now I have the basis of a plot for a new novel. I can't give away the plot here, I'm afraid, but it's going to make a really exciting book, believe me.

Having taken 14 years to get close to finishing my first novel, I hope that some shortcuts might be available if I write my next book based on her dream. Perhaps she can download a chapter at a time in future dreams, or dictate to me in her sleep? Perhaps I can stick a USB cable in her ear and download the whole thing straight into my laptop? I love the idea that this whole book is already sitting up there in the cosmos waiting to be downloaded. Maybe that's how all inspiration occurs – we build a connection between our minds and a huge cosmic database of songs, poems, jokes, plays, sitcoms and novels? It's a lovely idea, but it could prove complicated for intellectual property lawyers.

Sample blog: Too many flashbacks

It's really important to start a novel well. And that's why I've rewritten the opening chapter to *The Sphinx Scrolls* many times. When I was working on the book back in 2001 I thought it would be cool to open the first chapter at the most dramatic point in the early part of the story – with the heroine facing execution. This inevitably necessitated a number of flashbacks to explain how she had come to be in this predicament, but the structure seemed to fit the situation because it was like her life was flashing before her eyes. So far, so good.

Things got messy during the more recent rewrites. I wanted to introduce a juicy subplot and add more depth to the novel, and this required more flashbacks in that opening chapter. Trouble was, the new scenes were jumping back all over the place in terms of location and chronology, and I had found myself with a first chapter that had become too long and too confusing.

I decided to extract the opening chapter and put it into a separate Word document. I knew it needed major surgery, but in case things went badly wrong I had the original version to return to. But if things went well I would be able to transplant the new, improved chapter in place of the old, rambling one.

The next step simply involved putting every jumbled up part of that chapter, flashbacks and all, into chronological order. I didn't know if it would work that way, but at least it would tidy everything up and give me something easier to work with. That didn't take long, just ten minutes or so, and as soon as I read the story in the correct order I realised how much the flashback technique had compromised essential detail. Parts of the story had been glossed over too quickly, creating a lack of credibility in places. Now I had a chance to build the story on stronger foundations. I decided to rewrite the first page entirely from scratch.

An hour passed. I had a sentence on the screen. Another hour: another sentence. Time for a break. Two sentences in one morning had exhausted me. Bearing in mind these were to be the first lines of the novel I didn't feel that I'd wasted any time. It had been tough. I wanted my novel to open succinctly and memorably like *The Day of the Triffids*. I rejected line after line, word after word, until something started to emerge that I liked.

After lunch I ploughed on with page one of the novel. Soon I had a whole paragraph. Wait – no, I had to scrub a line that didn't work. The book went backwards for a while. Time passed while I researched the details of the scene on the Internet. I even watched clips of Guatemalan breakfast television to make sure I described everything correctly (I've never seen such a long-winded and pointless weather forecast for a country that's always hot). Suddenly the lines were flowing again. I was achieving my goal of a more subtle, mature writing style. It was a huge improvement on the words I'd written ten or more years before. Into the third writing session of the day and I was getting a decent word count for this new chapter. By the time the electric guitar riffs of *Top Gear* dragged me away from my computer I had contributed almost a thousand words to the novel. No flashbacks so far, just an elegant introduction to the main character as she slowly becomes aware that all is not well in Guatemala City today.

The rewrite of chapter one was completed and I think it's true to say that scarcely a single line of that opening chapter was retained from the previous draft. It reads like a new book, and a far more interesting one at that. I cut about five thousand words from the old draft, and I don't miss a single one. The fresh writing style of this new chapter carried over into the rewrites of chapters two and three. The story is now awash with new ideas, twists and surprises and the prose is imbued with elegance and maturity. Having found 'my voice' I'm finding it easier to push ahead into the next chapters.

[And you know what? A year later I scrubbed that entire new chapter and started again.]

66 *Write for the most intelligent, wittiest, wisest audience in the universe: write to please yourself.* **99**

HARLAN ELLISON

TWITTER AND OTHER SOCIAL MEDIA

Writers want to be read. We thrive on the satisfaction of knowing someone, somewhere is enjoying our words. Twitter provides an opportunity to broadcast pithy lines to anyone who cares to follow our tweets, and is like a miniature version of a blog. With a smartphone you can broadcast your tweets from anywhere. It seems that the more tweets you send out, the more people will sign up to follow you. Tweet about your writing efforts during the entire process of creating your work, and when it's time to market your completed project you can start by letting all of your followers know about it. A ready-made audience of loyal friends, fans and followers can kick-start the sales of a book, especially if they 'retweet' about it to their own followers. A fan base on Twitter is also worthy of mention to any publisher when you submit a manuscript, as it proves that people are interested in you and your writing.

Twitter is just one aspect of the ever-expanding range of social media that can be utilised to your advantage when you have something to promote.

You can spread your message by commenting on other people's tweets and blogs or by taking part in Internet forums. For example, if you are a non-fiction writer you can post comments, questions and answers on forums related to your specialist subject, making it clear that you are an expert and gently plugging your book at every opportunity. There are discussion forums on just about any topic on the Internet, and by adding your thoughts to these debates your name and expertise will be visible to those searching for years to come. It's also worth contributing to Wiki-based websites such as Wikipedia (sites where anyone can edit or write the content) to ensure that you, your skills and your writings are known to the world. And don't forget to take advantage of all that Facebook and similar sites have to offer – set up a page to promote each writing project and invite people to 'like' it. You can even post simple videos on YouTube and elsewhere talking about your writing and what inspired you. These self-promotion opportunities make many writers cringe: the transition from solitary author to being a social media star can feel uncomfortable and unnatural. But in today's publishing industry, the author's role in promoting themselves and championing their book is an essential part of every marketing campaign. Just about every social media opportunity is available to every writer for free. Those who take advantage of them will have a chance to be heard; those who dismiss social media may find they struggle to have a voice at all.

ONLINE WRITING EVENTS

Links to all of the writing events below can be found on my website, www.stewartferris.com.

National Novel Writing Month
National Novel Writing Month (NaNoWriMo) takes place each November. It's an attempt at inspiring people to get writing by encouraging them to commit to achieving 50,000 words during that month. The uplifting feeling you get from being part of this mass scribbling helps to keep you motivated, which is important because it's a tough target to achieve. If you're writing in what little spare time you're able to eke out each day, quality will have to be forgotten.

> NaNoWriMo is about quantity, about gaining momentum and enthusiasm for your novel by recording your word count online each night and seeing how you compare to other writers across the globe.

You won't have a complete first draft at the end of the month – unless you're writing a novella, a children's book or a Mills & Boon-style romance – but you'll have progressed enough to feel confident about being able to reach the end. Some writers meet up with other NaNoWriMo members during the thirty days to swap experiences, boost each other's morale and review their work. Writing 50,000 words in a month requires almost complete abdication of your social life, and it's helpful to remember that although you may feel isolated you're not alone in this remarkable endeavour.

National Playwriting Month

This is another November event, its goal being to encourage the creation of a first draft of a new stage play within thirty days. Screenplays are not allowed.

National Novel Finishing Month

If you're not exhausted by your efforts in November, December's goal is to complete your novel by writing an additional 30,000 words. I should point out, of course, that this will only result in the completion of your first draft. Redrafting and improving your book will take more than a month to complete.

January Novel Writing Month

The targets continue with this new year's goal of 50,000 words. But whereas November's event is aimed at the creation of new novels from scratch, this event permits writers to continue existing projects and is flexible in its word count.

February Album Writing Month

February is given to songwriting, with the goal of composing an album's worth of material during the shortest month.

National Novel Editing Month

March is the time for those rewrites, and this event encourages you to dedicate fifty hours to editing your 50,000-word manuscript.

National Poetry Writing Month

This takes place every April, and participants aim to write thirty poems in thirty days. Like the prose-writing events, it is open to anyone and there are no winners or losers – it is merely a motivational challenge that can inspire writers and create a sense of team spirit and shared adventure.

Script Frenzy

This is no longer in operation, but its goal of writing a hundred pages of script for television, radio, stage or screen during the month of April was an admirable one and is still something you could attempt alone.

April Fools

This is a writing event, in April obviously, where anything goes: any genre, any length – just write!

July Novel Writing Month

If November is currently too far away, this is a similar event to NaNoWriMo that takes place in July.

National Novel Writing Year

This site offers a year-long strategy to nurture your rough 50,000 words into something sufficiently polished to submit to a publisher.

Top tips for making the most of technology:

- Use writing software to help with plots, characters and layouts.
- Add detail to descriptions of places you haven't visited using Google Street View.
- Take advantage of the freedom to write anywhere that comes from using a laptop.
- Make the most of the dictionary and thesaurus functions in your word processor.
- Download free books to assist your background reading from Project Gutenberg.
- Research facts and figures online.
- Assess the commercial viability of your ideas using the Internet.
- Promote yourself by writing a blog and using social media.
- Benefit from a sense of comradeship by taking part in online writing events.

6

TECHNICALITIES OF WRITING

BASICS OF WRITING A NOVEL

'There are three rules for writing the novel.
Unfortunately, no one knows what they are.'
W. Somerset Maugham

How many words is a novel?

The absolute minimum is 50,000 words – at this length it's bordering on a novella, for which the commercial market is tiny. Aim for between 70,000 and 150,000 words. You can check the approximate length of your favourite and most inspiring novel by counting the words on a typical page and multiplying the result by the number of printed pages in the book.

How to prepare for the challenge of writing a first draft of a novel

A journey of a thousand miles starts with a single step, as the saying goes. It is generally beyond the capacity of the human mind to contemplate vast distances or lengthy challenges, so we need to break them down into bite-sized chunks. A typical novel of, say, 100,000 words is too great a quantity to think about in its entirety. Divide the total into realistically achievable daily word targets and suddenly the challenge loses its requirement for superhuman powers.

Writing 500 words a day, five days a week gets you to the end of the first draft of 100,000 words in about ten months. A significant achievement attained with apparently insignificant effort.

An analogy might be: how would you prepare for a car journey of 10,000 miles? Well, you don't. But most drivers travel that far each year simply by clocking up a few miles every day. The mental preparation for writing a novel therefore relates to establishing a writing habit and forgetting about the Herculean aspect of the undertaking. The routine of writing will get you there. My routine involves chapters: I immerse myself in just one chapter at a time, and because they are fairly short I get to celebrate the completion of each one with satisfying regularity. Stay focussed on the sentence or paragraph you're working on at any point in time, and eventually you'll sit back and realise you've achieved a goal that to many outsiders seems almost impossible.

The difference between commercial fiction and literary fiction

These are unfortunate terms because they imply that commercial fiction is somehow not literature and that literary fiction doesn't sell. This may be true in some cases, but there are plenty of exceptions. Commercial novels are those which have plots that can be described succinctly, where the story is paramount and the book is written to appeal to a broad audience. A steady, if not brisk, pace is crucial, and the deepest recesses of the souls of the characters tend not to be visited.

> Literary fiction is more experimental, often trying new structures or original devices for telling the story. Literary writing is more artistic, sometimes closer to poetry than to prose.

The descriptive language might be more evocative and detailed than in commercial fiction, and the plot is more likely to focus on the turmoil within a character's heart than on car chases and conflicts. Instead of a plot and a couple of subplots, a literary novel might explore various themes in subtle ways, attempting to make a point about the human condition. Both types of fiction are commercial in the sense that they are published and sold alongside each other, but the opportunities for authors of literary works are fewer than for commercial fiction simply because the readership is smaller.

Most of my advice for novelists is based on the principles of writing commercial fiction and its subgenres such as crime, fantasy, science fiction, romance and thrillers. However, it doesn't hurt to aspire to the greater artistry of literary fiction and if you can nudge your writing in that direction you could end up with a commercial book written to an exceptionally high standard.

Description

When you write a novel you're creating a world, moulding people, making decisions about everything including a person's love life, the architecture, even the weather. You are omnipotent in your personal universe. If your setting is another period in history or a remote planet, you'll need to bring that place alive with your description. You're painting a canvas in your reader's mind. They see what you allow them to see, and that should be just sufficient for the context of the story to make sense, to have credibility and richness, but not so much detail that the story fails to move forward. Even if your setting seems a familiar one, such as a group of people in the present day in your home town, you still need to include the same depth of descriptive detail to make the story come alive. Not all your readers will be from your town, in any case. To readers on the other side of the world your mundane setting will seem exotic.

With every new location in the novel you need to set the scene. Remember to use different senses in your description. Most writers can describe what something looks like, but better writers will immerse the reader in the smells, sounds and textures of the place. Elements of the scene that are described in this way should be carefully chosen to create a feeling of time and location. Objects in the scenery and their condition and context can be used to symbolise themes in the book, just as the weather can provide a dramatic backdrop to your scenes.

Reader's question:
I've put a lot of local detail into my novel.
Is it going to be too parochial to be
of wide interest to readers?

Every novel needs a sense of place, and that place doesn't always have to be well-known cities like New York, Paris or London. Readers like to be taken to locations they haven't necessarily visited. It's fun to get the flavour of a locality, to learn of the idiosyncrasies and turns of phrase of its inhabitants, to get a sense of the landscape, architecture and climate. That's a far more tempting prospect than setting your book in a generic 'Anytown' avoiding specific details of place. So don't be afraid of being parochial: it didn't do any harm for Thomas Hardy's career, after all.

Characters

Don't just think of a name and a description and put words into the new character's mouth. This results in flat, drab writing. As a writer you must always be on the lookout for interesting characters in real life. Use people you meet for inspiration. If you end up at a party full of strange people with whom you have nothing in common, don't be disappointed – be thankful for the opportunity to note their eccentric characteristics and speech patterns for future writings.

Good writing stands head and shoulders above the rest when every character encountered has a life, a vocabulary and an agenda of their own. Even minor characters have been living their lives up until the moment they appear in your writing, and they don't want to give those lives up and simply join in the main story without a fight. Every little character must have their own ambitions and needs that will often be in conflict with those of the main character. Life is like that, and fiction in all its genres benefits from fully rounded and individual characters on every page.

Show, don't tell... Show, don't tell... Repeat this mantra every time you sit down to write. It means that you mustn't tell the reader everything about your character and their situation with direct description. Use the drama of the story and appropriate details to show the reader things that they will interpret for themselves.

If a character likes to rebel against authority, don't tell us. Show us. Show the bad attitude, the can-kicking in the street, the rule-breaking. If a character has a crush on another character, don't tell us: show it with their body language, their heavy breathing and the double entendres in their speech. Showing instead of telling is a mark of elegant and mature writing. It's one of the first indications that an editor can use to distinguish between a publishable work and an amateur work. Learn it, chant it, use it.

Unusual Character Names

When it comes to picking a name for a fictional character, why be boring? I like to use names that in some way reflect their personality, or which have symbolic meaning. It's also fun to use memorable names that make your characters stand out from the crowd.

The ultimate accolade for a writer is to have a character who becomes recognisable globally just from the mention of their first name. Think Ebenezer, Zaphod or Cinderella. If you can create characters with that kind of impact, you'll be doing well. Here are some great sources of interesting, original and unusual names:

1. A dictionary of baby names (the good ones will also provide the origin and meaning of the name)
2. The Bible or other religious texts
3. Any novel by Charles Dickens
4. The works of Shakespeare
5. Roman emperors
6. Greek philosophers
7. Children of celebrities
8. People's online pseudonyms
9. World leaders, especially dictators
10. My eBook, *Unusual Character Names for Writers* (which also contains suggested nicknames by which other characters might refer to them)

Reader's question:
Can I create a character that shares my name?

Why not? The character can be based precisely on you, or be similar to you, or simply share the same name. But think carefully before using the names of other people in your work. The rules about libel vary between countries, and at the time of writing the somewhat antiquated British libel law is undergoing a review in parliament which might result in some fundamental changes, but essentially you could be at risk of being sued for defamation if you write fiction that uses someone's real name. It is, rather surprisingly, possible to be sued even if you change a person's name. If that person is still recognisable from their dialogue, physical description, actions and context, and if it can be shown that what you've written may have harmed their reputation or business interests, then watch out. I faced such a conundrum in a novel I was writing: an earlier draft of the book featured a character based on a well-known government official in Egypt, the head of antiquities. He wasn't exactly an A-list celebrity, but within the archaeological world everyone knew his name. So I changed his name, but I realised that it was still obviously based on him because my character had the same attitudes and did the same job. So then I thought some more about it and decided to change the sex of my character to a female, and instead of conflict arising from the (relatively) well-known attitudes of the real head of Egyptian antiquities I hit upon the idea of my female character having been at university with the novel's heroine, and they had hated each other ever since. Having resolved this problem to my satisfaction, and to that of any Egyptian lawyers who might have studied the text, it then turned out that I had to say goodbye to this character anyway because I changed the ending of the book. But it was a useful exercise in solving the problem of the recognisability of real people in fiction.

Chapters and plot structure

Fiction permits a looser structure than many other writing genres, but you still need to make sure the reader doesn't fall into a coma trying to drag weary eyes across your turgid prose. When writing fiction, our instincts are to round off a scene to its natural conclusion, tidy up any loose ends, and then declare the chapter finished. Well, that was always my instinct when I started out, anyway. I liked to tidy things up, to have chapters that resolved the issues and dramas that they contained. And that attitude resulted in some pretty dull fiction. I realised during an early draft of a novel that the book was about as gripping as a weather forecast. There was no sense of jeopardy, of wonder, of the mystique of unanswered questions and unsolved mysteries. Not all types of fiction need these things, of course, but all novels should at least hold the interest of the reader and one of the simplest techniques for doing so is to end the chapter before the events therein are resolved. If a character faces a dilemma, such as being on the brink of making a difficult decision that will affect the course of their life, show the build-up to the moment of decision and then end the chapter before telling the reader what happens. If you can then delay the resolution of that scene until at least a chapter later (which means the next chapter should focus on a subplot) then so much the better. You have just initiated an overpowering desire in your reader to keep reading, and as a writer would you ever really ask for more than that?

One of the best modern examples of a good plot structure is Dan Brown's *The Da Vinci Code*. It's a very simple concept that owes much to the cliffhanger style of the traditional Saturday morning cinema. You take a story and then break away from it at just the moment when the reader thinks they're about to learn something crucial. Cut to a second story thread and run that one for a few pages until something interesting seems about to occur then leave it floating in mid-air while you bring the reader back to the resolution of the first story's cliffhanger. Then create another moment of suspense and cut to the other story. This simple structure occurs throughout the novel, with the result that the reader is perpetually keen to read on and resolve every little cliffhanger along the way. The chapters are reasonably short so there's no potential for getting bored.

This novel is a phenomenal success because it achieves the rare feat of being read right to the end by just about all who buy it. They get to the end quickly, they enjoy every twist along the way and they recommend it to their friends. I'm not saying that every novel needs to be written using the same structure as *The Da Vinci Code*, but you need to understand how bestselling novels are constructed before considering your own plot structure.

If it's necessary for the reader to know the back story that occurred in your characters' lives before the main plot began, don't delay the start of the real story by detailing too much historical context. Start the story at an interesting moment where there is conflict or life-changing decisions to be made and then work the back story gently into the plot as you progress. This doesn't have to be through flashbacks: it could be through the reminiscences of two characters who meet after a long separation; via the accusations that fly out during an argument; or in the answers to questions posed by a psychiatrist to a patient.

How do you know when a chapter is long enough?

Your chapter will reach the requisite length at precisely the same time as the apocryphal piece of string.

The content of your book is a world of your own creation. You are omnipotent. You make the rules and you can break the rules. You can have a chapter that's just a word long, and you can have one that's a thousand pages long. This is an artistic endeavour and you must follow your instincts as the all-knowing, all-powerful creator of that art. And whilst all of the above is true, I would not recommend that you pay any attention to it if you want to get published. Listen to me at your peril! (The first bit of this section, not the most recent bit. You know what I mean.)

When deciding on the length of a chapter, consider three things:

The flow of your story
There is a rhythm to every book. It can be ultra-fast paced, it can be slow and leisurely, or it may flit between the two, grabbing the reader by the neck and dragging them along for a bumpy ride and then letting them rest a little before picking up speed again. As the author you need to be aware of this flow of energy. Is it time to change the pace, to switch to a subplot, to leave your hero in peril whilst you cut to a different scene, knowing your reader will be salivating to discover what happened to him and won't be able to turn the pages fast enough?

Your reader

How do you think your reader will feel if you write a chapter that continues unabated for a hundred pages? Readers rarely tackle a book in one sitting. A chapter break is a convenient place for the reader to pause. It gives them the satisfaction of having completed a quantifiable chunk of reading. My personal preference is for short chapters.

> When I write fiction I aim for somewhere between 1,200 and 1,800 words per chapter.

It's enough to establish the setting, get the characters interacting, throw in the event that will make the chapter interesting and propel the story, and to round off with a little twist or cliffhanger. It's based on my experience as a reader, preferring chapters that I can digest easily in a short reading session, with the option of reading for longer without having to worry that I might become stuck in a seemingly unending chapter.

Your potential publisher

Here's where it comes down to commercial common sense. Whatever genre you write in, it helps to be aware of the books with which you might one day be competing. How long are their chapters? Is there a typical, average number of chapters in a book? If so, you'll be doing yourself a favour if you try to write chapters of similar lengths.

Reader's question:
I want to put some of my own experiences into my novel. Is that a problem?

It's more likely to be a problem for you if you *don't* dig deep into your experiences and emotional repertoire. Some of the best writings are those that come from the author's heart rather than just their imagination. Turning your memories into scenes, characters, dialogues and descriptions can bring your writing to life, with intricate details and deeper insights that will connect with the reader. At a more basic, practical level, writing from your own experiences helps you to think of something to write. Fictionalising a major incident in your life can also be a therapeutic process, helping to come to terms with past trauma and emotional scarring. You can write about yourself and people you've known as much as you like in your fiction, with the only caveat being the requirement to respect the privacy, reputation and legal rights of others in order to avoid potential lawsuits after publication.

To plan or not to plan

Is there any point in inserting a new thread into a story if you don't know exactly how it is going to play out later in the book? It appears to make sense to take the time to work out exactly when and where this new storyline will appear and how it will affect the main plot and the characters. But I know from my own experience that in a novel of more than 100,000 words I simply can't calculate the intricacies of those events in advance. Instead, I have a tried and tested system of redrafting that involves the introduction of a new theme, followed by a systematic edit

TECHNICALITIES OF WRITING

sweep of the whole novel during which I bring in instances of the new theme wherever it seems appropriate, and I adjust dialogue, actions and plot devices as I come across them.

When I get into a routine of daily writing I find that the book comes alive in my head to the extent that complicated plot situations resolve themselves while I'm driving, having a bath or even fast asleep. It's not unknown for me to wake up with a new twist or scene to add to the book. So sometimes the impact of a new theme in the story can be arrived at subconsciously.

Characters speak to me when they are fully developed. They each have their own voice, their own vocabulary: great characters have sufficiently distinctive turns of phrase that you know who is speaking without being told. Changing a theme or adding a subplot requires alterations to the dialogue, but well-rounded characters are very helpful in dictating those changes themselves.

Reader's question:
I want to write and I have ideas for a story, but what if I can't think of an ending?

All writers differ in the way they plan their stories. Some are able to plan every stage of the plot such that writing the full-length work is almost a case of joining the dots. Personally, I struggle to see too far ahead. I might have a vague concept of where I'm heading, but if my characters are strong enough they tend to forge their own way and trigger their own ending. That applies to individual chapters in fiction, too. It's all very well making a note that a certain event should occur at the end of a chapter, but once the characters come to life within the scene and start to act in the only way they can according to the personalities I've given them, they might push events in a different direction.

If you want the comfort of knowing the ending before you get there, here are some basic options that might help you to decide how to wrap things up (feel free to pick and choose or ignore them altogether):

1. The hero or heroine heads off into the sunset (or towards an unseen second adventure) having resolved all conflicts.
2. A subplot thread woven into the story earlier returns at the end either to save the day, to create a final hurdle to be overcome, or to wrap things up comfortably.
3. The use of a prologue and epilogue can create the feeling of a tidy ending, wrapping the plot in an 'envelope'.
4. A new problem is encountered by the protagonist at the end – this will remain unresolved, but will form the basis of a sequel.
5. The themes in the book come together at the end to reveal something profound about the protagonist or about life in general.
6. The story could just stop.
7. The use of a twist in the story can surprise and shock the reader or viewer – but make sure it is justified by planting seeds that lead to it earlier in the work, don't just bring in something utterly random at the end.
8. Ambiguity can be thought-provoking, so rather than wrapping things up clearly leave a little room for personal interpretation. But beware that too much ambiguity can make people suspect that you didn't know how to end it.

Reader's question:
I want to write but I don't think I'm clever enough to write a whole novel. I get frustrated by having to rewrite and by the long time it takes to write something. Is there any point starting?

I want to play in the Wimbledon tennis championships but I'm not very good at tennis and can't be bothered with all that practising needed to become good enough. I want to win *The X Factor* but I don't have a great singing voice and the hours of rehearsal needed to become competent puts me off. I want to be a cordon bleu chef but I'm hopeless beyond cheese on toast and find it boring trying to improve my kitchen skills. There are plenty of other options on this planet: sometimes we have to choose wisely and recognise when our aspirations are unrealistic. If you don't have the determination to persevere at something challenging, don't set yourself up for failure and disappointment: simply choose a more suitable path. If you don't think the novel genre is your thing but you still want to be a writer, what about short stories? What about poetry or articles or local guidebooks? But having said that, no one is born with the ability to write a decent novel. We all have to learn that skill, and if you can overcome the frustration at having to rewrite and can get into a routine that helps you to forget the vast period of time it will take to finish it, then the novel remains an option for you.

Reader's question:
I want to write a novel – should I do it in the first person or the third person?

I used to find writing in the third person quite challenging: describing the inner thoughts and feelings of characters from a detached position of omniscience seemed complicated, and it was hard to maintain a mature and elegant style. I then edited and published a novel by another author who had written it in the first person, and I wished that I'd started my own book in that way too. This first person novel was full of insights into the protagonist's mind, and it all flowed with effortless grace. But the inherent restrictions of the first person may not suit all types of novel, and actually it wouldn't have enabled me to tell the story I wanted to tell. Maintaining a single perspective throughout a novel adds a layer of complication to the act of plotting and writing that risks leading your story to a dead end. Only write in the first person if you have a clear idea of your route to the grand finale so that you can be sure there will be no holes in the story.

" *It is a delicious thing to write, to be no longer yourself but to move in an entire universe of your own creating.* **"**

GUSTAVE FLAUBERT

Top tips for writing a novel

- Aim for a target word count that is appropriate to your chosen genre.
- Don't be overwhelmed by the task ahead: break it down into small daily targets.
- Use all of the senses in your description. Be specific and detailed, rather than generic.
- Give all your characters their own goals, challenges, and an 'arc' through which they grow during the story.
- Pick interesting names for your characters.
- Consider whether a 'cliffhanger' ending to your chapters is appropriate to your style of book.
- Study the structure and chapter length of published books to get a feel for whether your chapters are an appropriate size.
- Don't worry if you find it difficult to plan your entire story in advance. Ideas will come to you all the time, and there arc plenty of opportunities to enhance the story during the redrafting process.

66 *There are no laws for the novel. There never have been, nor can there ever be.* 99

DORIS LESSING

BASICS OF WRITING
SHORT STORIES

The physical constraints of a short story (somewhere between 1,000 and 20,000 words, but most commonly in the range of 2,000 to 5,000 words) mean that the writer needs to focus on a single event rather than a complex plot. This could be a turning point in a character's life, the big moment when everything changes.

Your reader needs to feel that they have chanced upon this character at the most interesting moment in his or her fictional existence, to feel privileged to have witnessed an epiphany, a tragedy, a maturity or the final minutes of comfort before stepping into the unknown.

Short stories don't have to follow any kind of structure – they can be a slice of life, they can start in the middle of an event and stop before any resolution is revealed, they can finish with a twist or they can represent a moral attitude. If you write short stories for pleasure or in the hope of getting a collection published or self-published, you have complete freedom with regard to style, structure and length. If you want to be published in a particular magazine, or you're writing for potential radio broadcast or for entry into one of the many competitions that exist for this genre, then you'll need to pay close attention to the rules and restrictions of your intended recipient (which will vary widely, but each of them will set their word length and topic and any other criteria on their websites) and make sure your subject matter and word count are appropriate.

66 *After nourishment, shelter and companionship, stories are the thing we need most in the world.* **99**

PHILIP PULLMAN

BASICS OF WRITING
FLASH FICTION

Also known as short short stories, sudden fiction and microfiction, this is a genre that contains any stories too diminutive even to be considered 'short', which in practice usually means stories written in about 300 to 500 words, with a maximum of about 1,000 words. The extreme economy of word usage required to tell a tale in this format means that the reader will often be required to infer meaning from the clues presented to them. There isn't room for characterisation, landscape description, back story, subplots or much dialogue. Flash fiction is a good term for the genre because it's like trying to tell a story by flashing an image at the reader.

If you look at a photograph in which a man is running with a woman's handbag and a woman appears to be distressed, you know the story. It's possible to tell that simple story with a single visual image, and that's what you have to do in flash fiction.

BASICS OF WRITING NON-FICTION

Know your subject

There are many more non-fiction books published each year than fiction. Novels may be high profile, but the bread and butter of the book industry is the range of non fiction subjects that occupy the majority of the shelves in a bookshop. Biography, science, history, self-help, sports manuals, recipes and travel guides are all non-fiction subjects. Most books in these genres are written by experts. But what is an expert? How do you become one? Actually, many more of us are experts than we realise. Once you have done a particular job for a few years you're an expert at doing that job. You don't need training to do it – in fact, you're capable of training new people to do what you do. Have you kept up a hobby over a long period? Fishing, photography, stamp-collecting... you're an expert in that hobby. Whether your field of expertise warrants a non-fiction book is another matter. If you feel you have something to add to the body of knowledge that's already out there, then you should try to formulate a new book.

Even if your expert opinions are similar to those already expressed by other authors you may still find a publisher willing to sign you up in order to enter into competition with books by other publishers on that subject.

So what if you have no expertise? How can you become one of those non-fiction authors who write books about subjects in which they are not experts? The answer lies in research. All the information that any expert needs is already out there in the public domain, either in books, journals, magazines or on the Internet. This wealth of raw material can be arranged into, potentially, billions of books. Anyone can access it; anyone can become a non-fiction author. Supplement that information by interviewing people who really are experts in their field. Then add your own interpretation and theories based on what you have learned. Hey presto: a new non-fiction book.

Structure

Many non-fiction books can be structured in a very simple way that makes them easy to write. My formula won't work with every subject, but it's worked on a number of occasions for me and authors I've employed. In fact, I've written several bestsellers using it.

Step 1:

Choose your subject matter and break it down into about ten chapters.

Example

You want to write a biography of John Lennon. Ten chapters in this book could cover:

1. Childhood

2. Art college and early rock music

3. The Beatles in Hamburg

4. Beatlemania

5. The psychedelic years

6. John and Yoko

7. Going solo

8. Watching the wheels: the New York years

9. Death of an icon

10. Musical legacy

Step 2:

Look at each chapter and divide
it into ten sub-chapters.

<u>Example</u>

Taking a chapter from the John
Lennon biography, Chapter 4 –
Beatlemania, you could divide it into
ten sub-chapters as follows:

1. John's involvement in
writing the first hits

2. The effect on his marriage to Cynthia

3. The psychological impact
of the fan worship

4. In His Own Write – John's book

5. The movie roles

6. The truth behind the 'Help!' lyrics

7. The pressure of constant touring

8. The backlash against his 'bigger than Jesus' comment

9. The evolution in his songwriting

10. The strains within the group

Step 3:

Write between three and ten paragraphs for each sub-chapter. The first draft of your book is now complete.

How many words is a non-fiction book?

There are no rules about word count for non-fiction in general – the rules will be specific to the genre and the publisher's requirements. Typically 20,000 words is enough for many kinds of smaller non-fiction book (the first edition of this book was about 23,000 words; this expanded edition is more than 50,000 words). Larger books can contain upwards of 60,000 words. A major political biography would be hard to complete in less than 100,000 words and could easily reach double that quantity. If the book requires illustrative content such as photos, diagrams, charts or line drawings, then in some cases it will reduce the necessary word count, depending on the publisher's requirements.

66 *You must often make erasures if you mean to write what is worthy of being read a second time; and don't labour for the admiration of the crowd, but be content with a few choice readers.* **99**

HORACE

BASICS OF WRITING FOR CINEMA

Cinematic writing is an exercise in minimalism. If you adapt a 120,000-word novel into a two-hour screenplay, you'll have to retell the story in less than 30,000 words. This is because cinema is a visual medium. The pictures tell the story. There's no opportunity to describe what is happening inside a character's head like there is in a novel (actually, you can do it, using voiceover, but let's not get complicated right now), so it's more important than ever to be able to show the audience what is happening. An agonised facial expression on screen might be the equivalent of a page of description in a novel in which the character's thoughts are spilled out for the reader.

Film also doesn't allow the luxury of long conversations that are frequently found in novels. The dialogue must be crisp and punchy. If the average length of a speech is more than two lines, then your script is in trouble. If your dialogue extends for pages and pages with no action, then again your film is too static and needs more action. By action I don't necessarily mean car chases or explosions. Action can be picking up a pen and playing with it suggestively. It could be an instruction for the actor to change facial expression or sit down. These things are tools with which to tell your story and are just as important as dialogue.

A correctly laid-out page of film script equates to about a minute of screen time, so the number of pages you need to write is the same as the number of minutes in a movie. Most feature films are 90 to 120 minutes long, so a script of 90 to 120 pages is the right length.

Commercial, successful films follow a formula that is very rigid. Most audience members in a cinema won't be aware of the structure, but once you know how the stories work you can predict plot twists almost to the second.

There's a free Word document that you can download from my website which contains the standard formula for a Hollywood movie. Just write your own story into the plot boxes according to the instructions.

Reader's question:
If I want my novel to be made into a film, should I write the screenplay adaptation myself?

Studios buy film rights to novels all the time, even without a script being written in advance, so it's not essential to write your own adaptation. But it's a great exercise to do because it will teach you what your novel is really about. You will need to trim scenes, characters and especially dialogue by as much as 80 per cent in order to convert your book into a standard-length screenplay, and this process will highlight sections of the novel that are mere padding or scenes that head off from the main story at a tangent without contributing to the core plot. You might then be able to redraft your novel as a much leaner, tighter and fitter book, which will increase its readability.

Reader's question:
I'm writing a novel which I think would make a good movie. Could I adapt it to a screenplay by stripping out most of the description and keeping the dialogue?

I tried this method myself as an experiment and ended up with a script that was 600 pages long (a two-hour film requires 120 pages of script). So simply extracting the dialogue and adding some scene headers and acting directions does not turn a novel into a screenplay. I had to cut about 80 per cent of my dialogue in order to get the script down to roughly the right length. That process taught me a great deal about what is really important, because it was possible to tell the same story with a fraction of the original words.

66 *It is good to have an end to journey towards; but it is the journey that matters in the end.* 99

URSULA K. LE GUIN

BASICS OF WRITING
FOR TELEVISION

Writing for television is not just like writing for cinema but with shorter scripts. Budgets are lower, scene and cast numbers are more restricted, and structures, formulae and script layouts are different. With the vast explosion in numbers of television stations there are more openings for television writers than ever before, although many of these new opportunities will not lie in the scripting of new drama series or sitcoms. The demand for writers will be in writing voiceover links between shows, one-liners for chat-show presenters and narration scripts for reality documentaries. This kind of writing is difficult to do as an outsider. You need to be working in television in order to hear about and get the chance to write this stuff.

Usually there's not much point writing an episode for a television series currently airing. That series will have finished production long ago and the team will have disbanded. Writing a sample script for a long-running soap opera might open doors for you, however. But don't waste your time or theirs by writing something that wouldn't fit smoothly and naturally into the existing line of episodes, and don't attempt it until you've watched the soap actively for a few weeks (years of passive watching doesn't count!).

BASICS OF WRITING
FOR RADIO

The market for radio writing is very small and doesn't pay as well as television. Short stories, plays and series are all broadcast on radio. Short stories for radio need not be any different from print, but radio drama is a fundamentally different challenge for a writer. Imagine writing a play for the stage, then blindfolding the audience after they've sat down to enjoy the play. The set disappears. The actors are invisible. The movements, expressions, props and lights cannot be seen. Your story must now be told entirely through words and sound effects. This requires a different kind of dialogue in which an image of the characters must come through without compromising the realism of the speech. The colours of the landscape around the characters must be painted in sound. You can use echo in a voice to represent an empty room or a cave, or have a backdrop of the sounds of street noise or ocean waves, birds, dogs, wind and rain. The mere presence of other people must be mentioned if they don't have lines to say, and any lines they do say should hint at their identity and role.

Aim for a balance of sexes and accents so that there are clear distinctions between the characters. Much radio drama suffers from the blandness of the sound effects: slamming doors, feet on gravel, telephones ringing.

Douglas Adams set out to transform the potential of radio sound effects with his groundbreaking original radio series of The Hitchhiker's Guide to the Galaxy. If you think the medium of radio drama is restrictive, then listen to some episodes from this series to hear an example of what can be done with sound alone.

66 *You can't wait for inspiration. You have to go after it with a club.* **99**

JACK LONDON

BASICS OF WRITING
FOR THE STAGE

I wrote a two-act play at university. It wasn't anything that Shakespeare would have been proud of but it was my attempt at writing a deep and serious psychological thriller. So when it got more laughs than a sitcom I was a little surprised. The minor witticisms I put into some of the characters' lines would scarcely raise a smirk if read in a book, but there was something about the intimacy of the stage and the connection the audience makes with the actors that seemed to elevate the words beyond my original intentions. I realised that writing for the stage is different from any other genre because it's the only form of writing that can become truly alive for the audience. Film, radio and television are artificial forms of life. You can't make eye contact with the performers. Books are flat, static. The only life they bring is in your imagination. But plays for the stage have a unique immediacy and humanity that ensures the medium has remained popular in spite of a hundred years of film.

Many new plays are 'workshopped'. The writer attends sessions with the actors in which scenes are tried, ad-libbed, themes explored and suggestions made so that the writer can go away and formulate a script. Joining a theatrical group is the best way to get a play performed. I've also been involved in a play that was workshopped in this way and the director wrote the script from ideas generated in the ad-lib sessions, while I wrote the songs according to the direction the play was taking. Some workshops start with the writer's script, then through a process of rehearsed readings the script gets torn apart and the writer is sent off to put it back together again according to their wishes.

It's very hard to write a play and find a theatre willing to show it. Before you start, watch as many contemporary plays as you can. Discover which theatres are showing the kind of play you'd like to write, and keep that venue or stage layout in mind when writing. Be aware of budget – as a first-time writer you can't expect a cast of thousands and a hundred scene changes. Stick to three or four actors and one or two simple sets. Put up your budgetary boundaries before you begin to write and then create something special within those walls. That's the kind of thing many theatres would like to see.

When writing a play remember that it's a live medium. Not all audience members will be in the line of sight to spot a facial expression or hand gesture. The set won't be fully realistic and there has to be a degree of suspension of disbelief. And the audience has paid money and made the effort to travel to the theatre to be entertained, so entertain them!

BASICS OF WRITING
BOOKS FOR CHILDREN

This category covers a wide range of age groups and types of writing. Every age group has its own fiction and non-fiction books. Before you start any writing project for children you must know the age range of your target readership. The conventions, vocabulary and style for each age group will vary so do your homework and read plenty of current books aimed at that market. Depending on your age it might not help to read the stuff you enjoyed when you were a child: attitudes have changed since then, and much of it wouldn't get published today. Besides, modern children are far more technologically proficient and sophisticated than in previous generations, and the concept of 'family' is far broader than it used to be, so their reading materials need to be fresh and relevant to their lives and experiences.

The youngest children's age groups consist entirely of illustrated books, while older children will read books with few if any pictures. If the real selling point of your book is going to be the beautiful artwork that you imagine running alongside your text, then it would be wise to team up with an illustrator at an early stage to create a joint project, unless you are a competent artist yourself. Children like to read about other children, not adults. Make your heroes children of the target age group, and make sure they solve the mysteries and overcome the odds on their own rather than with adult help. It will make kids identify more with your characters and want to read every book you write.

Don't forget that adults make many book purchase decisions on behalf of their children, so your book may need to appeal to them. And for younger age groups, it's the grown-ups who are going to be reading the book aloud so anything you can do to entertain adults at the same time as the main audience will be most welcome. One way to do this is to write on two levels, with a clear and obvious story for the children and the occasional nod and wink to make the adults smile (and by 'nod' and 'wink' I mean subtle jokes that only older readers would appreciate, references to themes or problems with which only adults would identify – this is the literary equivalent of a gentle nudge to let them know that you're thinking of them whilst they read your story).

Do as much objective testing of your story as you can. Read it to any children you know and try to note points in the story when their attention starts failing. These are the bits where you need to add twists and surprises to maintain the enthusiasm of the children.

It helps to read the latest school curriculum to see what children are already reading as part of their education, and to find out what words and knowledge you could reasonably expect kids in your target age group to understand. Look also at the bestseller charts in the bookshops and online to spot the new trends in publishing for young people. Try not to talk down to children. Give them relevance and excitement, an imaginary world where they can create adventures because the kids are in charge, not the grown-ups.

BASICS OF WRITING POETRY

What separates poetry from prose (prose being every other type of writing described in this book, not to mention this book itself) is hard to define. Think of the words in their adjectival forms, however, and it's easier to sense their meanings. If something is 'prosaic' it's pedestrian, drab, plain and unembellished. Think of the word 'poetic' and you begin to imagine beauty, artistry and something that has been created with emotion and perception.

> *A poet is an artist who paints with words, and, like art, poetry can take many forms, from traditional to avant-garde.*

Poetry has certain formats for which conventions apply, such as limericks, sonnets, epigrams, blank verse, haikus and dozens of varieties of rhyming patterns and half-rhymes. It's fun and it's good practice to experiment with creating poems within the strict boundaries of a particular format: then, when you decide to break out of those restrictions and write free verse, you'll have a keener appreciation for that freedom.

The absence of rules for writing free verse doesn't make it easier to write good poems. Putting a mirror up to a part of the world, or to your soul, or to your emotions takes sensitivity and care. Finding a fresh and original angle via which to present an everyday scene or situation takes imagination. Choosing the right words to convey your thoughts takes economy and discipline. Poetry is your private method of expressing your take on humanity. Your style will evolve naturally the more you write. Your poetic voice will become a window into your heart.

BASICS OF WRITING COMEDY

Although comedy can be taught, the best way is to develop a natural sense of humour as a result of being bullied at school for some minor physical deformity and finding that if you make the bullies laugh they won't beat you up so much. There's nothing like the threat of a bunch of fives to accelerate the learning process.

What makes us laugh? Have you ever wondered why some things make you laugh? Have you noticed that watching a comedy show more than once reduces the amusement you gained from it? I think the lesson here is that one major source of laughter is the surprise element. It's not enough just to be surprised by unexpected things suddenly appearing on the screen, otherwise we'd all be in hysterics watching horror movies. There has to be something more, some kind of cerebral association between what we're seeing and what we already know (what has already been set up – characters, incidents, knowledge) and that connection should be made without warning.

The comedy writer takes us along a path in our heads that we think is familiar and suddenly drags us down a side alley where we make a link with something that makes us laugh. You'll probably never laugh again having had humour analysed like this, but if you want to write comedy, you need to understand the importance of unanticipated connections. Feed an idea into your audience and turn it on its head. Surprise them, twist them, build on the initial gag by referring back to it later on. Often the second or third twist on the same subject gets a bigger laugh than before.

Sketches

These usually fall into two kinds: situation based and character based. *Little Britain* was character based. You could stick those characters anywhere and they would still be funny. *Smack the Pony* was situation based. You could put any characters in those situations and they would still be funny. When there's a long-running sketch show on radio or television there can sometimes be openings for new writers. Watch or listen to the credits, find the production company and look up their website. Send them your sketches, but make sure you write the sketches for that series specifically.

There are theatre groups that perform regular satirical comedy shows, sometimes in seedy little venues in pub basements. But they're perfect breeding grounds for new comedy talent, and just hanging out with them and offering them your work is a great way to get started and meet other writers.

One-liners

The market for one-liners is small and specialist, and tends to be fed by an inner circle of comedy writers. Topical one-liners are used by some radio and television presenters at the start of their programmes, and by stand-up comedians.

> A one-liner is a joke that consists
> of one sentence in two halves:
> the set-up and the twist.
> I'll tell you the easy way to make a million
> in publishing... start with two million.
> That's the kind of thing.

If you want to write one-liners, you'd be well advised to do some stand-up yourself to test out the material. Sometimes there will be a television or radio show that accepts satirical one-liners from outside writers for its weekly broadcasts, so keep an eye out for those rare opportunities.

Sitcoms

Sitcoms are deceptively difficult to write. They look like the easiest thing on television to emulate, especially when so many are pretty awful, but in fact it's the toughest skill to master. There are many professional comedians doing stand-up comedy in the clubs and testing jokes and material on real audiences, all of whom are trying to get their original sitcom commissioned. There are also thousands of people in other walks of life desperate to be sitcom writers. That's many thousands of sample scripts being written in an attempt to fill a handful of television slots every year. And still there are bad sitcoms being made. That suggests to me that the skill of writing good sitcoms is beyond most writers, and television producers have to make do with second best just to keep working.

All sitcom dialogue has to serve one of three functions: character development; plot development; or laughter. If a line cannot be said to fall under any of those categories, it should be cut. Ideally a line of dialogue will fit under two or three of the categories at the same time. But don't be tempted to think that all of the laughs must emerge from dialogue: what isn't said can be far funnier than the words on the page. A character could respond with a look that brings the house down. The sudden appearance of a character, unseen by another who is busy trashing their personality, is a tried and tested technique for laughter.

In America the sitcom industry works with large teams of writers, enabling a sitcom to be produced week after week for many years. Often this results in a low standard of television sitcom. What do I mean by this? Surely these sitcoms generate lots of laughs per minute? True, the number of laughs per episode is very high, and that's a natural result of dividing the script between many writers. These writers all depend on generating laugh after laugh to justify their jobs, so they play out hundreds of different punchlines before deciding which is best, and they do this many times on every page of every script. But it's hard to do this in a way that reflects a character in any meaningful way, so in my opinion many American shows written like this simply provide a large number of shallow laughs from unrealistic lines shoehorned into the mouths of unconvincing characters.

I'd rather have a sitcom with fewer laughs provided that they were much bigger ones. But how can you get proper, full-on belly laughs out of a sitcom audience? How can you make them laugh so much it hurts? You need good foundations for your sitcom. Firstly, your characters must be believable. They can be stupid and daft, eccentric and bizarre, but they must have basic human qualities, needs and failings with which the audience can identify. Without these characteristics they are merely two-dimensional gag machines. Secondly, your plot must be carefully and intricately constructed to ensure that laughter emerges by the truckload at certain key twists and turns in the episode.

Admittedly, the American sitcom writing system produces some classic series that retain their quality through a hundred or more episodes. A British sitcom will have a shorter lifespan, fewer episodes and fewer writers. When this system works it can outshine anything produced by the American writing factories, but when it fails, which it frequently does, it makes producers start to consider switching to the American way of working.

The essential thing to remember with a sitcom is that it is a situation comedy. Writers who interpret the word 'situation' to mean the 'setting' will not produce a funny script. The setting is the office, the bar, the family home, the hotel, or whatever backdrop the characters share. There is never anything inherently funny about a sitcom's setting, nor need there be. The comedy comes from two things: the characters, and the situations in which they end up. Characters can be funny without any story, but that's little more than stand-up comedy. The best sitcoms make the audience care about their lives, their minor tragedies and fears.

To create a funny situation in a sitcom requires a great deal of work on the characters and the structure. The structure of the plot can't exist in a vacuum: everything that happens must be the only thing that could happen given the combination of characters involved. Basil Fawlty can only hide the truth about a guest who died in the night. That is his character and the rest of the plot inevitably results from that. *Fawlty Towers* is often held up as an example of the best sitcom ever written, and this is with good reason. Every one of the twelve precious half-hour episodes took six weeks to write at a time when other sitcom writers would churn out an episode in just two weeks. Writers Connie Booth and John Cleese treated each episode like a short play, in particular like a farce in the style of Molière. There were no constant one-liners – sometimes there would be no laughs for the first minute or two of the script, but the clever plots and twists that put the characters in funny and painful situations built up into laughs that were so big they would hurt. It was a situation comedy in the proper sense, where the laughs came from believable characters who ended up in situations where we could only laugh at them.

David Brent in *The Office* digs similar holes for himself to Basil Fawlty, but in a more subtle way. If the audience believes in and cares about the characters, then the pain they feel is all the more real, and a surprising amount of comedy comes from the emotional pain that our favourite characters suffer.

Comedy is not an easy concept to describe because it's not an exact science with immutable laws. How funny a gag is perceived to be depends on a joke's geographical and sociological context, the delivery style and the audience. Victorian political satires won't send us into paroxysms of laughter today. Paul Merton kept a straight face when telling jokes because he discovered the laugh received would be twice as big. An audience of students will laugh at different things to an elderly audience.

I'd never recommend comedy writing to anyone who doesn't have a natural predisposition to be witty. There are links to more information on the basics of writing comedy on my website, www.stewartferris.com.

Reader's question:
I want to write something funny but what if not everyone shares my sense of humour?

A humorist with universal appeal? What an appalling prospect! There isn't a comedy writer on the planet who can tickle everyone's funny bone, thankfully – if there was, the result would be a watered-down, lowest-common-denominator, insipid style of comedy. And that would undermine the concept of universal appeal anyway. Part of the charm of cutting-edge comedy that pushes the accepted boundaries of taste and taboos is knowing how shockingly unfunny some people will find it, and that makes it all the more funny to those who do enjoy it. We all have varying attitudes to what is funny, and although you may be able to entertain a majority of your audience, you'll find that differences in age, sex, class, culture, beliefs and life experiences will trigger reactions to the same joke that range from hilarity to indifference to outright anger. But it's a big enough world for you to be confident that your own sense of humour is not unique. There will be others out there who will enjoy sharing the comedic lens through which you view things. If you can develop a consistent style and gain a reputation for a particular brand of humour, then your like-minded audience will follow you, and those who are not turned on by your comedy will stay away. Be thankful that not everyone shares your sense of humour, because for those who do it's like being in an exclusive club where all the members are on the same level intellectually, and their passion for your work will be heightened by the exclusivity they perceive.

BASICS OF WRITING
FOR ANIMATION

If you have an original concept for a cartoon series, it's not going to be easy to sell it to a production company or broadcaster without sample drawings and preferably a sample of the animation itself. Animation is even more of a visual medium than cinema. Most of the gags are visual. There may be several layers of comedy happening at once, with the dialogue, the main character's amusing actions and the mayhem happening in the background. It's not easy to get this kind of visual storytelling across in a written script, but every show is different. *SpongeBob SquarePants* began life as amusing doodles. It's an artist-created show. The visuals came first, and a top-rate script came after. But other cartoons are written first, animated later.

Writing for an existing cartoon show means getting to know the characters inside out. When I started writing scripts for *Pokémon*, there had already been five television series and six films before me. The kids I was writing for were familiar with the back story of the characters and with the conventions of the show. I needed a crash course in everything *Pokémon*. I watched every episode I could find, I read the books, looked at the websites, and met the actors. I attended the dubbing sessions, when the voices are added to the video, to learn everything I could about the show and how it was put together.

Animation has the potential to go way beyond the other entertainment media. Nothing is impossible in this genre. You create your own rules of physics and life and you use that freedom to build wacky adventures for crazy characters. Just remember that you're doing it for the kids, in most instances, and the tone will vary according to the precise age group for which you are writing.

> If you're writing something like *The Simpsons*, then you've got to make kids and adults laugh at the same scenes. Not necessarily at the same bits of each scene, though. The beauty of these top family shows is that many layers of humour and meaning are often happening at the same time. Which elements make a viewer laugh will depend on their level of maturity.

66 *If you can't annoy somebody, there's little point in writing.* **99**

KINGSLEY AMIS

BASICS OF WRITING
FOR VIDEO GAMES

The storyline is an essential part of the appeal of some video games. Someone has to write those stories, and if you're familiar with the modern gaming world and have ideas for creating new games, or for future incarnations of existing ones, it's worth getting in touch with the gaming producers with your proposals. Unfortunately, there are very few openings for writers in this market, so luck is going to play a major part in obtaining any work. You'll need to prove to a gaming company that you have the ability to come up with multiple, flexible, interweaving storylines that still make sense whatever decisions the player makes.

66 *I admire anybody who has the guts to write anything at all.* 99

E. B. WHITE

BASICS OF JOURNALISM

Journalism is the ultimate business end of the writing industry. No time for faffing and procrastination. No time for endless redrafts with lengthy breaks in-between. No opportunity for unlimited creativity and imagination. Journalists have to work to simple but essential rules:

1. Speed. When writing a news item, it has to be new. News is a highly perishable product: people don't want it when it's old, and it can expire in as little as a few hours. If you're writing about something that didn't happen very recently, you'll need to 'hook' it to a current event in order to make it feel relevant to the reader.

2. Neutrality. Your job is to present facts (unless you write an 'opinion column', but that's straying from the essence of journalism) and you should do so from an unbiased position. Others may have strong opinions on the story you're writing about, so you can quote them in your report, but make sure you present both sides of the argument.

3. Remember the essential questions that readers will want answering in your item: who, what, where, why and how? Read any news story and see if you can spot those questions beneath its structure.

BASICS OF COPYWRITING

At the glamorous end of this business are the copywriters who come up with slogans for major brands such as foods, cars and airlines. These people work in advertising agencies, and there's little scope for contributions from freelancers at this end of the market. But have you thought about who writes the text for a local restaurant's website? Who comes up with the wording for the special offer leaflets that come through your door? Who creates the product descriptions in the catalogues of businesses in your area? Many of them will use freelance copywriters to give their marketing message the polish and pizzazz that only a professional creative individual can provide. You'll be expected to listen to their requirements, take their own rough draft as your raw material, and fashion phrases for your clients that are succinct, sexy and saleable.

... however great a man's natural talent may be, the art of writing cannot be learnt all at once.

JEAN-JACQUES ROUSSEAU

Reader's question:
How do I decide whether to write my story as a novel or a screenplay, a radio play or a television drama, a stage play or an extended poem?

Writers usually feel a passion for a particular format. They really want to write a novel or they really want to write poetry, etc. If you don't have that passion for one format or another, but you have an idea for a story, there are other considerations you could bear in mind:

1. Does your story contain technical requirements that would make it prohibitively expensive or complicated in certain formats? You might need multiple exotic locations, aircraft carriers, exploding oil refineries and specific weather in order to tell your story. So it's probably not best suited to the stage. Television executives are unlikely to be chomping at the bit to get hold of it, either. Novels, poetry and radio plays have no budgetary restrictions when it comes to scenes and locations, of course, so those formats are open to you. Finally, the screenplay format: we've all seen big-budget movies where it seems that anything goes, but for a first-time screenwriter you are more likely to sell a script to a small-time producer who is looking for something that can be made on a shoestring.

2. Are you more experienced or knowledgeable about one format in particular? Each has its own rules, customs, layouts and requirements, and it's a steep learning curve to undertake each time you tackle a format for the first time. Scripts are especially rigid in terms of layout and length and

it's essential to be familiar with these restrictions and to work within them if you want to have a chance of commercial success.

3.   Is there enough in your story to sustain a lengthy work such as a novel or a feature film? Is it better suited to a short story or a short film, perhaps?

4.   Is your story full of introspection, action or dialogue? Although any of these styles can be moulded into any format of entertainment, introspection (particularly where the story revolves predominantly around a single character) is easiest in the novel format; action deserves the big-screen format; and dialogue is perfectly suited to stage and radio. Most stories combine these elements anyway, but if you suspect that one of them may be dominant then consideration of the choice of format before you start could make the project easier to complete.

❝ *Forget all the rules. Forget about being published. Write for yourself and celebrate writing.* **❞**

MELINDA HAYNES

BASICS OF GHOSTWRITING

This is a specialist niche that covers fiction and non-fiction, and involves writing a book for someone else. Typically a celebrity obtains a publishing deal for their memoirs, and the publisher or the celebrity will hire the services of a ghostwriter to create the text. The ghostwriter will use extensive interviews and materials provided by the celebrity in order to be able to carry out the assignment. Celebrity branded novels can also use ghostwriters. In some cases the writer receives no credit in the publication, but in others they may see their name in small letters prefixed by 'with', after the name of the celebrity.

Top tips for writing non-fiction and other genres

- Study good examples of your chosen genre. Read books, scripts, poems – but read hundreds of them, and do so with an active mind, noting their structures, patterns, rhythms, stylistic devices and tones.
- Follow my formula for writing non-fiction books if it suits your subject matter.
- Length is crucial to most kinds of scripts, so pay close attention to the number of correctly formatted pages you need to write.
- Writing for children means first choosing a specific age group and tailoring your style to that audience.
- Not all comedy appeals to everyone – develop your own comic style.

BROADENING YOUR LITERARY HORIZONS

Writing groups

It's good to expose yourself and your writing to the friendly and sympathetic environment of a local writing group. Early in my writing career I attended a writing group hosted by a woman who was a published novelist with a selection of impressive-looking hardbacks sporting her name. The group met in her house and discussed their own projects, and she would set writing tasks for everyone to complete and then read out so that others could offer help and guidance. Even though everyone there had profoundly different skills, styles, ambitions and potential it was a valuable experience because it was a microcosm of the real world. One day real people 'out there' are going to read your writings, criticise them in private or in public, misinterpret and misunderstand you, and fail to enjoy the subtle layers of irony you spent so long lacing into the text. Better to receive that criticism early on, from your compassionate writing group, than from a vicious journalist with the power to end your writing career prematurely with one merciless review.

Use a writing group as a sounding board to test your ideas and skills, but a time will come when you won't need the hand-holding and encouragement that they can offer. When you reach that stage it's because you're no longer an amateur: you've become someone who can host their own group and help new writers with the benefit of your experience (and that's a character arc!).

Writing classes

Classes are more formal than writing groups. There's more emphasis on the technicalities of writing, such as grammar, layout, character and plot. Choose a class that's tailored to the kind of writing you want to perfect. Learn the specifics of writing for the stage, or comedy sketches, or technical manuals. You'll progress more quickly by specialising.

Graduate and postgraduate creative writing degrees

Creative writing graduate and postgraduate degrees are becoming more widely available than ever. Some courses specialise in certain kinds of writing, such as novels or screenwriting, others give training in a wide variety of creative writing genres. But would such a qualification count for anything in the real world? Do publishers and producers value and respect them? I think they do. If they don't like your work, then all the qualifications in the world won't persuade them to buy it. But the point of studying creative writing is to be able to produce work that people will enjoy reading. If the course teaches you the commercial realities as well as the technical and artistic aspects of the subject, then it's going to point you in the right direction. You'll be well on your way to writing like the professionals. You may even gain some contacts and have the opportunity to network whilst on the course. Your tutors may come from significant sectors of the market that you're hoping to sell to.

If you think a degree in creative writing might be right for you, try to find someone who has been on the course and ask if it was helpful for them. Find out as much as you can about the courses you're considering. How much opportunity to write does the course contain? Will you come out of it with a finished novel or screenplay? Any course that gets you writing every day with guidance and feedback from professionals can't be a bad thing.

Writing alone or writing with a partner?

This is an individual choice. Writing partnerships are common in television, film and radio, and are often found creating non-fiction books. Teamwork seems to benefit all of these genres, but there are just as many examples of successful solo writers as there are partnerships. One advantage of working with someone else is that it puts pressure on both of you to come up with the goods on time. No one wants to let the team down, so writer's block tends to be driven away much more quickly. It's good to have the sense that the project is progressing faster and to have someone's hand to hold during difficult times. But there's only half the money waiting for you when you make it big...

It's very unusual to see a writing partnership in fiction. Novels are such individual efforts and the writing voice is always unique to the writer, so it's something that most people don't even attempt. But there have been notable successes, such as the novel *The Rule of Four* by Ian Caldwell and Dustin Thomason.

Top tips for broadening your literary horizons

- Use a local writing group as a sympathetic sounding board for your writing style.
- Writing classes can accelerate your progress towards mastering your chosen genre of writing.
- If you have the opportunity to study for a creative writing degree, do it. You won't regret it.
- Consider teaming up with a writing partner if it suits your genre and style.

7

GETTING
PUBLISHED

PUBLISHING IS A BUSINESS

'You must keep sending work out... you send that work out again and again, while you're working on another one. If you have talent, you will receive some measure of success – but only if you persist.'

Isaac Asimov

Publishing companies can only exist if they can make a profit from books, and that profit is not simply determined by the quality of the books they produce. It also comes from the demand for a particular book or author – books that are high quality and books that become bestsellers are not always the same titles. Another factor that determines the publisher's profit margin is how many staff are needed to edit the book and to deal with the author.

A book that is not written using a word processor will incur extra costs for the publisher (see the chapter 'Preparation for being a writer' for more on the correct writing tools to use), as will a badly edited book and an author without an email address.

It's unlikely that a potential bestseller would be declined due to any of these factors, but you won't be doing yourself any favours by presenting a manuscript in a less-than-professional way.

Reader's question:
How likely is it that I can get published in printed book form?

Statistically speaking, not very likely. The odds are against you. Millions more books are written than are published. Each time a book is released commercially, a publisher has risked substantial amounts of time and money to create and market that product. They can't risk those sums on every manuscript that comes their way: they have to pick very carefully from their submissions to ensure that they can be confident of getting the best return on their investment. But those cold numbers shouldn't stop writers from trying. The odds can be strengthened in your favour by following the redrafting rules in this book, by researching publishers to make sure you only submit to companies that are interested in your kind of book, and by ensuring you follow the publisher's submission guidelines and present yourself and your manuscript in a professional manner. You can increase your chances further by using social media to create a platform to promote yourself as a brand, to let the world know about your writing and to generate a following of friends and fans.

LOGLINES, SYNOPSES, TREATMENTS AND SAMPLES

As if it weren't hard enough having to write thousands of words at a professional standard, you also need to be your own publicity and marketing department and come up with the phrases and summaries that will sell your work. This is a skill that is often neglected by writers, and yet it's actually more important than the work itself. It's like the cover of a book: if it's an awful cover, potential readers won't be tempted to pick it up and read what's inside. I know from bitter experience that books I've published with poor cover designs will not sell no matter how good the writing is. People really do judge books by their covers. The way in which you pitch your writing to a publisher is just the same as that book jacket. You don't need pictures or design, just punchy words that will sum up the essence of the writing in an intriguing way to make the reader want to read the full work.

A logline most commonly applies to screenplays, but it's a useful thing to have for any creative work. It's a summing up of the main theme in one sentence, the shorter the better (although not quite as short as you see on movie posters – they can afford to be just two or three words because the picture is telling the story instead). It works in a similar way to a book's subtitle, explaining a little more than the title itself is able to do. When I co-wrote a humorous travel book, *Don't Mention the War*, we decided the book needed a subtitle to explain what it was about. We settled on A Shameful European Rail Adventure, which summed up the book in the fewest possible words.

A logline (or tagline) gives your story a focus, a distilled essence, and that simplification is a helpful way to introduce the values and aims of the story to those who are unfamiliar with it. Ultimately it can assist publishing executives, sales teams and bookshops to carry your message to those who matter the most: your readers.

A synopsis is usually about one page in length and summarises the story succinctly. A treatment does the same job, but adds more detail and runs to about five pages. Finally, the samples of your work will usually be between one and three chapters of a book (or about fifteen pages of script). Samples don't have to consist of the first chapters – you can select the best bits from within the body of the work if you think they do you justice.

Reader's question:
I have already designed the cover and done the page layout for my book. Surely that will help me get a publishing deal because the publisher won't have to do much?

I've seen plenty of cover designs and supposedly typeset pages from authors over the years, and there are usually a few main problems with them:

1. They don't match the specifications for the publisher's page sizes, margin sizes, typefaces and general house style.
2. Even a well-written book has to go through an editing process with the publisher, and there's no point in typesetting the pages until that process is complete.
3. No cover design ever submitted to me along with a manuscript has ever been used. Publishers have firm sets of criteria that they use for their cover designs, based on their

experience of what sells in the market place. They may also have specific branding requirements or a general 'look' that they are trying to achieve.

So don't bother. It doesn't gain you any advantage, and if anything it makes you stand out as unprofessional. Publishers have systems in place to get books typeset and covers designed. The system works. It's what they do. What you do is to write. Don't try to do their job for them. Are you going to offer to chauffeur the managing director around, make the tea, arrange their Christmas party and choose where to get the book printed? It's just not necessary. They can manage all that without you. The only thing they can't do is write a masterpiece. That's the one part of the publishing jigsaw for which they need you. You do your bit and let them do theirs, and everything will tick along nicely.

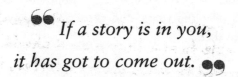

**"*If a story is in you,
it has got to come out.*"**

WILLIAM FAULKNER

HOW TO SUBMIT YOUR MANUSCRIPT

'Literature is an occupation in which you have to keep proving your talent to people who have none.'
Jules Renard

Before submitting your work to any publisher, you should always check their website to see if they have specific requirements for submissions. Some may insist on seeing a sample by post or by email. Others may be happy to receive the full manuscript in a big box, while others may accept nothing unless it comes from an agent. Don't annoy them by doing anything other than what they request.

Read other books by that publisher and think about what those books contain that may have encouraged the publisher to sign them up. Would your book fit in well amongst them?

An experienced editor will normally be able to see that a book should be rejected from its covering letter, title and first page. This is a combination that's so easy to get right and yet so many new writers let themselves down by displaying a lack of confidence, professionalism and common sense.

Printing your manuscript on gold-leaf paper won't make anyone want to publish it if the words it contains aren't up to scratch. If anything, it would set you at a disadvantage because trying too hard with the manuscript presentation is a sign of an amateur. Let your words speak for themselves by printing in black ink on white paper, using the layout appropriate for the genre and the publisher. Never use a manuscript twice: always print a clean copy for each submission. If your toner or ink is running low, make sure you replace it before printing all those pages. Publishers don't want to read weak and smeary text.

Keep your covering letter short, but don't neglect to mention anything that's relevant to the potential sales of your book. If you run a society for cat lovers with 500 members who could reasonably be expected to buy your book *Why I Love Cats* when it's published, then mention it. If you're about to appear in a television documentary and would have a chance to mention your book, tell the publisher. If your best friend is the editor of a newspaper and has guaranteed to review your book favourably, make sure the publisher knows. Anything you can do to make a publisher confident that they won't lose money by publishing your book will help them to make a decision in your favour. I was once about to reject a book that was perfectly well written but which seemed unlikely to generate sufficient sales to make it worthwhile publishing. Then I noticed in the author's letter, lost amongst a mass of irrelevant paragraphs, that he was offering to purchase a thousand copies of the book himself if we were to publish it. That was enough to swing my decision. We published the book. But remember, this was not a badly written manuscript – a publisher will not compromise their reputation for the sake of a quick buck.

> Wait a reasonable period before chasing the publisher for a response. It takes time to make publishing decisions. Books aren't picked on a daily basis.

Many rejections occur quickly, as do requests to see more of a book if only a sample chapter was received initially. Once the full book has been submitted, if there's a glimmer of hope for it then meetings are held at which the book is discussed, various people will need to read the manuscript and report back to the editors with their opinions, sales people will be consulted, and new budget allocations will have to be waited for. Then the manuscript may get lost, and then found, and finally a decision will be made. That decision will either be a rejection or an offer. This process typically takes three months.

Should you submit the book to other publishers during this period? It makes sense, otherwise if you get rejected at the last minute by ten publishers before signing a deal it will take thirty months to get there. It's common for agents to submit books to more than one publisher at a time in the hope of generating a bidding war between them. If you try this yourself, you must be honest with the publishers concerned. They won't be happy if they spend months discussing a book and researching its market potential only for you to email them and say it's been bought by someone else.

> For more information and insider tips about getting published, see my book *How to Get Published*.

Reader's question:
I want my submission to stand out from the rest. Should I use coloured paper and inks, and maybe wrap it in a fancy envelope?

No, no and no. When an author tries to do that, subconsciously I feel they are trying to distract the publisher from shortcomings in their work. Such a submission risks putting the publisher in a suspicious frame of mind from the outset. It's not what the professionals do, so don't do it if you want to be perceived as a professional writer.

Reader's question:
I've written a series of books. Should I send just one to the publisher, or all of them?

A series of books is an attractive proposition for a publisher. If they go to the trouble and expense of investing in you as an author, it's helpful for them to be confident that you're not a one-hit wonder. If your first book does well, the publisher will usually want to follow it up with a sequel or a related title. But it's not necessary to overload the publisher with the full text of every book when you make your initial submission. Follow the publisher's submission guidelines in relation to how much of the first book to submit, and simply accompany that proposal with a succinct list of follow-up titles. A title and a brief paragraph describing each additional book should suffice. Make it clear whether the rest of these books in the series are available to the publisher as completed texts or whether they are ideas or works in progress. It doesn't matter if the other books only exist in your mind at this stage: the fact that you have the vision and intention to write a whole series is a major plus point from the publisher's point of view.

Reader's question:
Should I tell a publisher about other things I've written when I submit a manuscript?

Yes and no. It's all a matter of proportion. Keep it relevant and if you can't keep it relevant, keep it brief. A publisher wants to know about things you've written that are in the same genre as the book you're submitting. But if those other works are unpublished or haven't won any kind of accolade or prize then don't mention them. A measurable success in self-publishing, complete with genuine reviews, will count in your favour. The line has to be drawn somewhere, and if your other writings cannot be linked to any kind of objective third-party judgement of quality then keep them off your CV. If you do fall into this category, however, there's no reason not to submit them for publication, of course.

Reader's question:
There's a publishing company near to where I live. Should I make an appointment to see them about my book?

Is your book written in a genre that is likely to be of interest to this company? Study their website, get hold of their trade catalogue if you can, and check that your manuscript is a suitable proposition for them. If it's a close match, then you could consider making a submission. As to whether you should make an appointment, there's nothing to stop you trying. Chances are, however, that the answer will be a polite refusal and a request to submit your book via their preferred channels.

66 *If there is a book you really want to read but it hasn't been written yet, then you must write it.* **99**

Toni Morrison

RESEARCH YOUR MARKET

Publishers specialise. Make sure the company you're submitting your masterpiece to actually publishes that kind of book. A simple search on Amazon or in your local bookshop will tell you which publishers you should approach. Don't be put off if they already have a very similar book to yours: although they may decide not to crowd the market with closely related titles, it's equally possible that having had a success with one book they're looking for a suitable follow-up.

Reader's question:
I've written a novel and I'd like to get it published. What should I do now that it's finished?

First of all I would question whether it really is 'finished'? Is it merely a completed first draft? Writers commonly mistake the completion of a draft with finishing the job of writing the novel. It feels like such a major achievement to have reached the end of writing a complete story that you naturally want to share the result and to find out if a publisher will buy it from you. So make sure you read the section on redrafting in 'The secret of writing like a professional' before going any further. Chances are there is still work to be done on this book, and you cannot send it to a publisher hoping that they will finish it for you.

Assuming your novel is actually 'finished', the next step on the road to publication is to identify its genre and to locate publishing companies which already produce books in that same genre. Visit a bookshop or search on Amazon for novels that are as close to your own as you can find. Who publishes them? This is the smartest way to target the most appropriate publishers for your work. Try to identify as many companies as you can, because not all of them will permit submissions directly from authors. Next, visit the websites of those publishers to locate their submissions procedures. Most will state clearly how they want manuscripts to be sent to them (if at all). Follow those instructions and wait for the response.

If the only companies producing your kind of book are the major publishers that won't look at submissions unless they come from an agent, you will need to send your work to agents instead. Finding a suitable agent is not as easy as walking into a bookshop and looking on the shelves, but there are plenty of online listings to sort through. Just search for 'directory of literary agents' and you'll be presented with a selection.

66 *Better to write for yourself and have no public, than to write for the public and have no self.* 99

CYRIL CONNOLLY

NETWORKING

In an ideal world anyone could sit at home, write a book or a script, send it off, and if it was better than the other writings received by the publishers and producers, it would get bought instantly. Life works a little differently, though. Put yourself in the shoes of the owner of a theatre. You want to stage a play. Writers you don't know send you stuff every week. Sometimes you read it; usually you glance at it and put it aside. Nothing has really excited you from what you've seen so far. Some day you intend rejecting it all and taking the scripts that didn't have return postage attached down to the recycling centre. But at a party you meet a writer who gets chatting to you. Turns out you're both keen jazz musicians. You talk for ages before getting onto the subject of plays. You already have each other's trust. A few days later her script arrives in the post. When you read it you see that it's no better or worse than the stack of scripts currently blocking the light from your window. But you liked her. It would be fun to work with her. The script needs work and development, but why take a chance with someone you don't know when you can work with someone you think you're going to get along with?

See how easy it is for this to happen? And it does happen. Every day, in every part of the writing industry. The reason is that a producer develops a working relationship with the writer. So it's only human nature to want to work with people you like. Networking is about getting to meet the right people and forming friendships that will develop into working relationships in the future. Getting a personal introduction to a publisher or a producer at a party will more than double your chances of selling your writing. Even if they don't buy it from you they may be prepared to give you their expert opinion for free. I've met authors who have appeared on television or radio shows with me who I subsequently published. I've given my opinion on books submitted to me via friends of friends.

Use any legitimate tactics you can think of to gain access to the inner circle of producers and publishers. It isn't an impregnable fortress. They're nice people who live ordinary lives. If you're not in the same town as they are, travel. Find out where they hang out. Go to their offices for a chat, even if it's just with the receptionist: you might learn something valuable. If you can't get to their location, use the phone. People often phone me out of the blue for advice or to ask if I'd like to see their book. It takes courage to do that, but what's the worst that will happen? A brush-off is all you'll get if they don't want to speak to you. It won't end your career.

Go to international book fairs to meet publishers. The big European ones are in London and Frankfurt, and the American one regularly changes venue. Chat to the people on the booths. Find out what kinds of books they want to publish next year. Take their cards. Hang out at the parties in the hotels — the networking opportunities really begin when the wine starts to flow.

EXPLOITING INDUSTRY CONTACTS

It's human nature to prefer dealing with people we know to dealing with faceless strangers with names that are nothing more than words on a page. In this business we all need a dose of luck, and if you have a friend or a relative or a friend of a friend of a friend of a relative who works in the part of the media for which you want to write, that's the kind of good fortune that you shouldn't ignore. Using a personal contact isn't cheating because it will never be a guarantee of success, but it can help you in some or all of the following ways:

1. You may be able to find out what kind of projects the company is looking to sign up.
2. You may have access to information about the personalities and preferences of the people you need to impress with your work.
3. You can find out directly how best to format and submit your work.
4. You may be able to get your submission handed to the right people in person by your contact.
5. Your contact might be able to put in a good word for you, so that your submission is prioritised over others.
6. If rejected, you might receive more detailed and constructive feedback than other writers.
7. You may be guided towards other companies that might be better suited to your work.

Make full use of business networking sites such as LinkedIn. Use it to build up an online résumé of your writing and other experience. You can connect to other writers and join groups of like-minded authors, and if any of your contacts are linked directly to a suitable publishing executive, you can request a direct connection with them. Facebook also has a role to play in building networks with other writers and industry professionals. You can create a Facebook page based around your writing project and invite your contacts to 'like' it. This is a useful method of demonstrating to a publisher your ability and willingness to market your work.

Reader's question: I know a published writer. Should I ask for their help in getting my book to a publisher?

Getting your book to a publisher is not the problem: there is nothing stopping you sending your work to any company or individual you choose. Getting the manuscript read and taken seriously is the more significant challenge. Never be ashamed to exploit any shortcuts that may be available to you: other writers will do so, even if you don't. Personal contacts can make a difference, but don't expect a personal introduction to a commissioning editor to increase your chances of publication if your manuscript simply isn't up to it. You'll get a more thoughtful and helpful rejection letter than most, though, and that's a valuable resource in itself that will guide you when refining the next few drafts.

WRITING COMPETITIONS

Most genres of writing have their competitions, and you should aim to enter as many of them as possible. An online search will result in a list of writing competitions in order of their closing dates, so you can prioritise your writing accordingly. Usually the entry fees are low enough that it's not unrealistic to think about entering everything that has a category for your genre of writing, provided you have time to write all those entries, of course.

Crafting a polished short piece for a competition takes days or even weeks, and can interrupt the flow of your other work (unless your everyday project happens to be perfect as an entry in itself). So why is it worth getting sidetracked into something that is peripheral to your main goal? Here are some of the benefits of entering competitions:

If you win or make the shortlist...

1. Your reputation will be enhanced from the point of view of professionals in the industry.
2. Doors will open for you. Agents and publishers will take you more seriously. Some film producers will only consider submissions from screenwriters who have had success in competitions, for example.
3. It boosts your confidence to receive objective confirmation that you have what it takes.
4. You may be published or produced, depending on the competition prize, and/or a cash sum will be heading in your direction.

Even if you don't win...

1. The act of writing an entry is an excellent discipline that helps you to grow as a writer beyond your normal creative experience.
2. You may receive constructive, impartial feedback to help you take the quality of your writing up a notch the next time.
3. You have added another work to your private catalogue, and if you are confident in what you wrote and believe you were simply beaten by the sheer high number of other entrants, then you can recycle this work by entering it in another competition.

Reader's question:
How important is luck in becoming a successful writer?

It's a regrettable truth – and one which cannot be swept under the writer's rug – that a significant number of professional writers owe their position not just to hard work, study and persistence, but also to luck. Change the word 'luck' to 'random chance' and it makes more sense. All of our lives are subject to random chance, whether it be good or bad. When we first meet a partner, what are the odds of us both being in the same place (or on the same dating website) at the same time? Think about your non-writing job if you have one: what were the odds that it was advertised at the same time that you were looking for work? What were the odds of the home you live in being available at the precise moment that you were seeking somewhere to live?

Everything in life is governed by random chance, and we just have to try our best to make the more fortuitous events happen. It's 'lucky' when a writer first gets a book published, but that writer will, to some extent, have created the conditions for that luck to happen. They will have edited and redrafted their book to a professional standard, they will have researched the appropriate publishers or agencies, and they will have made the effort to let those companies know about their work. The writer has followed a process that can generate good fortune. Sloppy writing or lacking the confidence to send out your work for consideration won't generate your lucky break. You won't win literary competitions if you don't make the effort to enter them. You need luck on your side, but it will only be tempted to come your way if you provide it with the conditions it needs.

66 We are all apprentices in a craft where no one ever becomes a master. 99

ERNEST HEMINGWAY

DIY METHODS OF PUBLISHING

Vanity publishing

This has always existed alongside mainstream publishing as a method of seeing your work in print. A 'vanity publisher' operates by flattering the author with praise, even though they haven't necessarily read your book (I saw a letter sent to an author by one such publisher and the letter of praise was so generic it could apply to any novel ever written). A publishing contract (which requires you to pay them instead of the other way round) will arrive quickly instead of taking months or years. If your goal is purely to see your writing in print quickly, to be able to hold a quality, bound book with your name on the jacket, and to be able to consider yourself a published writer, then it's a perfectly legitimate service to use. A small number of copies of your book will be printed and bound for your personal use, and other copies of the book can be produced on a print-on-demand basis. It's entirely possible, in theory, for an author to make a healthy profit from a vanity publishing deal. Copies will be deposited with the national library official archives. Any bookshop can buy the book, and your local stores will usually stock it for you if you ask them nicely. If you are able to generate a large number of sales privately, you could end up doing very well out of it.

For most writers who choose a vanity publisher it isn't about profit, though. Chances are they won't recoup their investment, but they're happy to be in print. For them, for their family and for posterity, that's the most important issue.

Print self-publishing

This is a more modern approach to getting your book in print when you've had enough of publisher's rejections. You essentially become a publisher yourself, although you don't need to know anything about the business because companies exist that will do all of the book production work for you. This is not the same as vanity publishing, because the responsibility, ownership and decision-making lies with you. You can create your own publisher's imprint and logo, and choose precisely how the book will look and feel. For more information about self-publishing, see my book *How to Publish Your Own Book*.

Digital self-publishing

If the cost of getting your book printed is prohibitive or discouraging, look instead at digital publication. The opportunities for self-publishing online have changed dramatically and quickly since the first edition of this book appeared, and at the time of writing this update the market is still relatively young and is liable to evolve unrecognisably in the coming years. If recent history is anything to go by, companies will buy each other out, one will dominate the market until something better comes along, others will go bankrupt. So I'll mention some of the current market leaders, and I'll just hope that none of them will have gone 'puff' before you read this. For more up-to-date information I recommend visiting my website.

The process of creating an eBook version of your text is made satisfyingly easy by free software such as Mobipocket eBook Creator – just open your Word file, save as a 'web page' (this will be an HTML file), then import that file into Mobipocket and follow its instructions. Future generations of word processors might incorporate this function to make it even simpler. But there will always be a potential problem surrounding the cover design. A bespoke design that represents the essence of your book and still looks good when shrunk to thumbnail size is a tough thing for a writer to produce. Hire a professional designer if you don't have any experience in creating book covers. Once you have the cover image file, simply import it to the Mobipocket software and your eBook is ready to be created.

Always check your eBook in a reader such as Mobipocket Reader (a free download) or on a Kindle or other device before trying to make it available to the public. The conversion of text into HTML and then into an eBook format sometimes plays havoc with line spacing, and can result in a frustrating reader experience. Sometimes it's necessary to spend time getting it right by trial and error.

Other forms of eBooks can be created using other software: PDFs, EPUB, eReader (.pdb), iBooks, plain text files and plenty more besides. It's a complex, confusing and changing industry – some websites only sell certain formats of eBooks, and some are not accessible to the self-publishing individual. So I'm going to present a summary of a few of the many options open to self-publishers at the moment:

Kindle Direct Publishing (KDP)

Mobipocket builds eBooks that are a perfect fit for Amazon's Kindle Direct Publishing program, which at the time of writing is a major force in the eBook self-publishing market. Setting up a KDP account is quick and easy, and is open to any author who wants to make their eBook available on the Amazon websites. Once your eBook file has been created it takes only a few minutes to complete the necessary title information and upload everything to the KDP website. You can choose a royalty level of 35 per cent or 70 per cent (although if you select the higher royalty, Amazon will charge you a small fee for digital delivery of your eBook and will not let you set your price lower than $2.99). Once you've chosen your royalty rate and price your book is ready to publish. KDP staff will review your upload and, once approved (usually within a few hours), your eBook will appear on the Amazon sites. And that's it. You're a published author. Your book can begin to earn money, receive reviews, and climb the sales rankings. Your words can turn into cash.

Smashwords

In addition to being an eBook website in its own right, with a vast range of self-published titles, Smashwords can get your book automatically listed on other websites. If you follow its recommendations with regard to how to format your text prior to using their bespoke eBook conversion facility, you'll be able to have your eBook available in several formats and on sites including Apple iBookstore, Sony and others. It's almost a complete eBook solution in one website, although currently they do not have any integration in place with Kindle – this situation will hopefully improve in due course.

Lulu

Lulu is a hybrid site offering both print services for authors and eBook services. It pays fair royalty rates and lists your eBook on a couple of other sites beyond its own, including Apple's iBookstore. Lulu provides cover design and marketing services, and after a decade in the business it now releases 20,000 titles each month, so it's a mature player in this young industry.

Scribd

It's possible to sell books on Scribd, but it's mostly a portal for free documents and is a great place to start if you just want people to read your work and are not interested in monetising it.

App self-publishing

If your book has the potential to be produced in an interactive format, offering something more than just linear text, then it could be suited to conversion into an 'app'. At the time of writing this is still a relatively complex process which, although anyone can do it for little money, requires some computer programming knowledge. The Internet is replete with companies that will create an app for you out of your content, however, so for a reasonable fee you can make your words available in yet another format.

Audio self-publishing

Another publishing format to which the Internet is ideally suited is the downloadable audio file. Not all types of written work make sense when read aloud, but for novels and many kinds of non-fiction books the genre presents another opportunity to make your work available to the public and to earn a return for your efforts. With a reasonable quality microphone, some inexpensive audio editing software on your computer and a quiet room with plenty of soft surfaces to deaden any echoes, it's possible to create a clean voice recording at a quality that's good enough to sell. Hiring a studio and technician to produce your recording is an option, but it's unlikely to be economically viable given the number of hours needed to record and edit a lengthy book. But I've seen authors recording books in their spare bedrooms or sheds, hanging duvets on the walls to make the space acoustically neutral, and taking the time to learn how to use the editing software to create a marketable product for very little cost. The audio file can then be sold via their own website or via third party sites. If you want to do it the old-fashioned way, you can even produce CDs or memory sticks containing the files.

Will self-publishing help you to get a publishing deal?

Not necessarily. Some editors might prefer to see a bound book because it helps them visualise what their edition could look like, or they might like your impressive sales figures. Others, however, might be put off by the fact that your book has already appeared in the shops and may be concerned that you've tapped the market for yourself and there's nothing left.

There's a new trend amongst the bigger publishing houses towards looking at self-published books in the hope of finding a gem that they can take on. *A Year in the Merde* by Stephen Clarke and *The Sea on Our Left* by Shally Hunt are both examples of self-published books that became bestsellers when taken on by larger publishing companies.

You could self-publish on a limited scale purely with the intention of sending every copy to reviewers and other writers for their opinions and quotes and to send to publishers. Or you can print on a larger scale and become a small publisher in your own right. I started out by self-publishing a thousand copies of my first book. Now I've printed and sold millions of books by hundreds of authors. So beware of what you might be taking on by publishing yourself...

Top tips for getting published

- Remember that publishing companies are businesses that need to make a profit in order to survive. When considering whether to publish your book they are thinking about it as a commercial product, not merely a creative work.
- Your sample materials (covering letter, loglines, synopses, sample chapters) deserve just as much effort as you put into writing the book itself.
- Don't waste your time submitting your manuscript to inappropriate publishers: research your market and target them effectively.
- Network with publishers if you can and use any industry contacts shamelessly.
- Enter every writing competition you can. Any successes will increase your chances of publication.
- Vanity publishing is a way of seeing your book in print, but it's an expensive option.
- Self-publishing in print or in eBook formats is usually cheaper and comes with a chance of recouping your investment.
- If you simply want your words to be read, there are many routes to digital self-publishing that can achieve this goal for you quickly and at no cost.

THE NEGATIVE STUFF

Dealing with doubt from within

Becoming a writer is a brave step in itself. Letting someone read your precious work is even tougher. Are you mentally prepared for this step? Do you worry about exposing the workings of your creative mind? Do you doubt that you're really up to being a writer in the first place? I truly believe that almost anyone can become a good writer given enough time, determination and hard work. I also truly believe that most writers who make a living from it are not any more naturally talented than the next person. Writing is a craft that they have decided to master. It is quite proper for you to doubt that your first writing efforts will be any good. Do you think Julian Lloyd Webber's first scrapings on the cello were enjoyable? Of course not. He studied the necessary skills and became a world-class musician. Your first writings may well be the literary equivalent of a five year old with a cello. It's normal and nothing to be ashamed of. Don't doubt yourself because you can't get it right first time. Chances are your first novel will be painfully bad, your second will be average and your third will be publishable. It takes time and effort to master the craft of writing. Financial rewards are a long way in the future. The only rewards along the way are in the form of the inner satisfaction you feel in achieving your writing goals and becoming slowly more proficient at it.

Reader's question:
What if I never become good enough to sell my work?

It's a possibility that every writer has to confront, and it may come true in some cases, unfortunately. But if you enjoy the creative process, does it matter that much? Writing is not just about the destination: it's a wonderful journey.

Reader's question:
Is there any point writing something that no one ever reads?

Only you can answer this. You could argue that there's no point financially speaking, since an unread work won't earn any royalties. Equally you could argue that it's a waste of time from the point of view of making a contribution to humanity's collective culture. I would propose a different way of looking at those unread words, however. If you've written something that no one will read, then you will have come to that conclusion due to one or more of the following reasons:

1. You feel it isn't good enough and you're not confident that you are capable of rewriting it to a professional standard.
2. You have no idea whether what you've written could provide enjoyment to others and are frightened of giving anyone the opportunity to assess it in case their feedback is negative.

3. You are aware of the shortcomings of the work, but have come to regard it as part of your learning process, a vital step on the road to improvement. You know that your next work will be better than this, and even though the next one may also never be read, it's still an important contribution towards your growth as a writer.

However much you write that no one ever reads (my own stack of forgotten works probably runs to more than 200,000 words), always bear in mind point number three above. No one writes a masterpiece at the first attempt. Each project takes you closer to your goal. And, perhaps above all else, remember that you have achieved the greatest thing a human can do... you have created something.

I should add that in this age of digital publishing, the option of enabling your creativity to be enjoyed by a global audience is one that you can very easily exploit if that's what you want to do. You can't guarantee that huge numbers of people will read it, but there will always be someone out there who chooses to read your work provided you make it available to them.

Dealing with doubt from others

If people mock or belittle your attempts to write, or they read and criticise something that you know is unfinished with the result that your confidence is crushed, you have two options. Either avoid them or hide your writing (at least until it's been through enough drafts for you to be sure that it's good enough). If you scribble a first draft which you know can form the embryo of a blockbuster, don't let a non-writer read it. Someone who doesn't understand what a first draft is will not give encouraging feedback. They'll compare it in their heads to finished books they've read and of course your efforts will look terrible to them in comparison. It's a first draft, after all. They've only read published books that may have been through a dozen drafts. So make sure you keep your first draft to yourself.

Getting feedback

> *'No passion in the world is equal to the
> passion to alter someone else's draft.'*
> H. G. Wells

You've polished your work to the best of your ability. You can see no faults or weaknesses anywhere in the text. It is the best you can make it. Now is the time to get feedback from someone. It's the moment many authors dread. After months in the bunker secretly typing away they now have to stick their head above the parapet and risk being shot at. Exposing your treasured words to the truculent eyes of a professional is a terrifying prospect. That is why so many writers opt to show their work to friends or relatives instead. Encouragement, admiration and praise are the things writers seek at this stage, but coming from the wrong people those platitudes can be disastrous for your career, giving you false hope and an inflated perception of your current abilities (I say current because we all can improve as writers throughout our lives and if a work is not good enough, that needn't be the end of the matter provided you are prepared to put in the weeks, months or years needed to raise your game). The story of 'The Emperor's New Clothes' is a valuable reminder that a single objective opinion is more valuable than dozens of biased comments designed to make you feel good.

Objective feedback at a professional level comes in various guises:

1. You can privately hire an individual editor to work with you or to write a report on your work.
2. You can submit it to agents, publishers or producers and hope that, if they say no to it, the rejection letter will contain more than just generic boilerplate phrases pasted together by an intern.
3. You can ask any personal contacts you have in the appropriate industry for feedback, provided you can trust them to be honest about your work.
4. You can use a web-based editorial or feedback service – there are many of these, each specialising in different genres of writing.
5. You can enrol on a writing course or degree and ask one of the tutors if they would consider evaluating your work.

Not all feedback is relevant. Your writing may be designed to appeal to a particular gender or age group, and if someone who is not part of your target market offers you negative feedback it's not necessarily a bad thing. Try to find appropriate people to comment on it. Obviously if several people who you thought your writing would entertain display a notable lack of enthusiasm then the chances are they're right and you need to look very closely at your work in order to find ways to improve it.

How to cope with knockbacks

Having been sufficiently courageous to expose your writing to a professional, you then have to deal with their feedback. This is the moment that you need inner strength and determination because they will have recommended that you rewrite some or much of your work. You may feel your stomach twisting in tight knots. You may feel nauseous, hurt, or offended. You may feel you're not cut out for this life and the temptation to give up could be overwhelming. It's not technically a rejection, but it feels like one. This is a knockback, and it feels awful.

So take a deep breath. Scream and whine in frustration. Vent a little. Go for a walk and silently curse the world for not understanding your genius. Then sleep on it.

Slept on it? Now turn it on its head. This is a positive event. This is for your benefit. You've been knocked back because you were heading down the wrong path. The rewrites will put you back on the correct route towards creating the result that you dream of. The additional workload will seem frustrating, especially when you have to throw out treasured phrases and passages that you worked so hard to write, but you're not alone in this. It is part of the job. Writers write forwards and they write backwards.

Get used to it. I've even had to write backwards on this book, as the first draft of this edition was too long. Whether this is your hobby, job, career, vocation – whatever you call it, progress is not going to be uninterrupted. When you're absorbed in your project it's easy to lose the objectivity that can highlight problems in the text. The knockbacks you'll get from informed and intelligent critics will set you straight. Be grateful for the homework they set you.

Dealing with rejection

People drive different cars from each other, wear different clothes and eat different food. They also watch different films and read different books. There's never been any product or literary work that has managed to please everyone. If everything written appealed to every reader, the world would be a pretty dull place. I mention this purely to give you a sense of perspective when you receive the inevitable rejections to your writing: 'inevitable' because rejection is part of the learning process as well as part of the selling process. Negative feedback with constructive criticism can help you to remould your writing into a product that someone with influence in the market likes. It's not enough that your dentist thinks you should be published. You need to persuade a publisher of that fact.

The problem for all of us writers is that even when your writing is perfect and your manuscript is professionally presented you may still encounter rejections. When a publisher tries to sell a new book into the bookshops many of those shops will reject it. But this doesn't necessarily reflect any inherent flaw in the book, which may still go on to be a bestseller amongst those shops with the sense to stock it. Part of the reason for good manuscripts to be rejected is that most writers create their works of art in a vacuum, with little regard for what the publishers actually want. They then waste valuable time trying to hammer a triangular peg into a semicircular hole that's probably boarded up anyway.

For the average new writer it's not easy to find what publishers are looking for. They certainly won't benefit from a phone call asking if they can come up with a book on X by Y date for Z amount of money like some established writers.

> A writer who comes up with the apparently brilliant idea of a novel written entirely in rhyming couplets with twenty bonus recipes at the end is going to be highly disappointed by the rejections that will follow.

Although you don't have access to a publisher's editorial meeting in which they discuss what kind of books they want to look out for in the next season, you can be sure they won't be looking for rhyming novels with recipes. The way to be sure is easy. Go to a bookshop. Look at the shelves and how they are labelled. Where is the shelf that says 'rhyming novels with recipes'? Exactly. If the book doesn't fit squarely on one particular shelf, the bookseller won't know where to place it. And if the bookseller doesn't know where to place it, the buyer doesn't know where to find it.

Sure, you'd like to think your book will just go face out on those bestseller shelves near the front of the store, but the statistics make this very unlikely. High street bookshops of average size carry about seventy thousand titles in stock, and only twenty titles will appear on those premium shelves.

The only thing you can do is to look closely at the actual labels of the shelves, look at the books on those shelves and see how similar they are within each genre.

Commercial writing is not about art for art's sake. It's about creating a product that can be marketed and sold as easily and quickly as possible in order to create a profit for the publisher and the bookseller. Without that profit they can't survive, and they're looking to you to provide them with the raw materials for their next slice of profit.

So learn what you can from each individual rejection. Try to reread your work from the point of view of the person who rejected it. (And remember they rejected it, not you.) If they provided any feedback, it's vital to read the work with their comments at the forefront of your mind. Are they right? Can you think of a way to fix it?

They may not be right, of course. Your writing could be rejected for a number of reasons aside from its inherent quality. During many years as a publisher I've rejected books because they were similar to books that had just flopped, and I didn't want to risk losing more money with another book like it. I've declined books on the grounds that my acquisition budget is fully allocated for the foreseeable future (which meant that we'd run out of money and couldn't pay any more advances or print bills for a time). I've said no to writers because despite my personal interest in the book others in the company have persuaded me not to publish it. I've had to reject authors who are quite clearly mad and unprofessional in their approach and who would be too much effort to deal with. Sometimes the rejections have been because we had already decided to produce a similar book either in-house or using our existing author contacts. Or it could be that I'd decided on a change of direction and was no longer interested in commissioning new titles in a particular genre which I felt wasn't right for my company. I'm sure there are editors out there who have rejected books simply because they're having a bad day and want to take it out on someone. And don't forget, of course, that most books are rejected because they are simply not good enough to publish.

Laugh off the rejections. Frame them and mount them on the wall of your bathroom. When you're a bestseller they'll be priceless. And remember you're in good company – the company of virtually every other writer on the planet.

Top tips for dealing with the negative stuff

- Self-doubt is natural, but remember that it takes time to become a publishable writer. Anyone can make it given enough time and determination.
- Protect yourself from negative criticism by not showing your work to others until all of the redrafting has been completed.
- When you are ready to show your work, only do so to people who are from the intended readership. Any other feedback could be irrelevant and potentially hurtful.
- Any criticism of your writing can be hurtful, even if it is intelligent and appropriate. Take a few days to digest any suggestions of further rewrites. Eventually you'll look back and be grateful for the feedback.
- Rejections occur for dozens of reasons, not all of them necessarily connected to the quality of your writing.
- Rejection is part of what it takes to be a writer. Every writer who gives up following a rejection letter will remain unpublished. Success comes to those who pick themselves up and dust themselves down and try again. And again.

COPYRIGHT, AGENTS, CONTRACTS AND ROYALTIES

Copyright protection

Anything you write, provided it is original, is your copyright automatically and will remain so until long enough after you die that it needn't worry you. You don't need to do anything to copyright your work. In theory. But reality is never that simple, of course. There's the little matter of proof. Ideally you should be able to prove to a court that you were the first person to write it. That's not as complicated as it sounds and it doesn't need to cost you more than a negligible sum. The traditional method was to put a copy of your work in an envelope, post it to yourself, check that the date of the postmark is legible, and then leave it unopened until that fabled day in court arrives and you then produce your proof of originality. The difficulty with this method is that it's easy to reseal an old envelope and fake the evidence. So instead of (or in addition to) that old-fashioned technique I recommend the following steps:

1. Ensure that you write in your document that the work is your copyright. The copyright symbol © is a powerful and recognised way of saying 'Hands off my work!' This does not change or 'strengthen' its legal status, but it could work as a low-level deterrent, making potential infringers think twice before stealing your hard work. Clearly write your name and contact details together with the copyright notice.
2. Keep all of your notes, early drafts, deleted scenes or chapters. All of this is evidence of your creative process, showing the

progression of ideas as you developed the writing. If someone copies your finished work, they won't have it in any of its previous incarnations and would not be able to show the court any evidence of how the writing evolved.

3. Register your work with a copyright protection agency, either online or with a physical copy of the manuscript.

4. Use security settings if you upload eBooks to the Internet to make it harder for your work to be illegally copied.

Reader's question:
I want to start submitting my work but I'm worried – what if someone steals my ideas?

I'm worried about swimming in the sea in case a shark mistakes me for an hors d'oeuvre, but I still do it. The risk exists, yet it's small enough that it doesn't need to obstruct my admittedly limited aquatic interests. I won't pretend that the theft of writers' ideas never happens, but professional publishers and producers are not in the business of stealing. If every writer allowed this fear to prevent them sending their work for commercial consideration, nothing would ever see the light of day. Follow the guidelines I've listed in the section on protecting your copyright and you'll be as protected as a writer can be.

There's actually a powerful reason not to delay sending your work out once it's ready: if you wait, there's a fair chance that someone in the world has been working on an idea that's similar to yours and they may get there first. This is especially true if your writing is in some way inspired by recent events in the world.

Some publishers and producers may ask you to sign a disclaimer when you submit to them. This indemnifies them against possible legal proceedings from you if they reject your work but subsequently release something that appears unpleasantly familiar to you. Reading such a disclaimer for the first time may seem like they are asking for your agreement that they can steal your ideas and not reward you a single penny, but there is a sound commercial necessity in their request. Proposals arrive on their desk and in their email inboxes every day, and you have no way of knowing if they are already working with another author on a project similar to yours. They may choose to reject your proposal purely due to its similarity to something they have been developing for over a year. They haven't stolen your idea, they have merely been submitted the same idea twice, and unfortunately for you the other writer got in there first.

Agents

What are they for?
Agents are a filtering system designed to save publishers' time. They are usually experts in a particular field of literature or genre of writing and pride themselves on their reputation for spotting talent and only presenting to publishers manuscripts of a professional standard.

Do you need one?
No. You can still get published without one provided your work is of a high enough standard and is presented in a professional manner. However, not all publishers and producers are open to submissions from non-agented writers, so your potential market will be smaller.

How hard will they work for you?

Agents live off a percentage of your earnings. If they don't sell their clients' work, they don't eat. So it's in their interests to do a good job. Most agents will work very hard for their clients, but to do this they must restrict the number of clients to a small level. For an agent to take you on they may have to let someone else go, and that's why it's so hard for unpublished writers to find representation.

Contracts

What constitutes a fair contract for your writing? This is impossible to answer comprehensively, since what seems fair to one writer may seem utterly inadequate to another. You may be offered a fixed fee for your writing service, or you may be offered a royalty structure with some of your future earnings paid up front as an advance. There are approximate industry standards, of course, but how close you're able to get to those standards depends on your bargaining power. As a new author, that power is weak. As an established author with a proven track record, that power is strong. In simplistic terms, the more successful you are as a writer, the more publishers will offer you.

> **"** *No author dislikes to be edited as much as he dislikes not to be published.* **"**
>
> RUSSELL LYNES

Reader's question:
I've been offered a royalty of 12 per cent of the income received by the publisher for my book. Why should they keep 88 per cent of the money?

You invested time in the creation of your manuscript, and you deserve to be paid for that. The publisher has to make a more substantial leap of faith, however. They will invest considerable sums of money to edit the text and design the page layout and the cover, to produce the files needed for the print version of the book and any digital editions, to produce the marketing materials, to pay for the printing and transport of the printed copies, to pay the sales people and the warehouse company, and to pay a portion of the general overheads (office rent, wages, utility bills, local taxes, consumables, etc.) that are an inescapable part of running such an organisation. The publisher stands to lose money if the book doesn't succeed: it might be the case that the first 3,000 units sold represent a loss to the publisher, even when they retain more than 80 per cent of the income they receive. Only if sales continue beyond that level will they start to make a profit. That kind of risk requires a higher reward. You keep your advance, no matter how the book performs, so your cash is not on the line. Publishing deals vary in the detail, but the general principle that the author receives a small slice of the pie is universal because publishers simply need the bulk of the income to stay in business. Imagine if the percentages were reversed, with the author receiving most of the money... the publisher might then need to sell as many as 25,000 units to break even. Only a minority of books sell in that kind of quantity and your publisher would quickly go bust.

Royalties

How do royalties work?

A royalty is a payment made based on quantity sold or income earned. The old-fashioned method is to pay an author a percentage of the retail price of a book. The author would earn the same regardless of the discount taken by the retailer. But most publishers now adopt a more flexible approach by paying the author a percentage of the income they receive. So if the publisher makes less money from selling the book the author earns proportionately less, and vice versa. A royalty based on income should be a higher percentage amount than a royalty based on retail price.

Publishers normally send sales statements to authors and pay royalties every six or twelve months. Some writers receive statements reporting negative sales. This occurs when the number of copies sold in the accounting period is less than the number of unsold copies returned for credit by the bookshops. Often despite high sales there is no royalty paid. This is because the author has yet to earn back the royalty advance.

Royalties can be a fixed rate, or they can be based on a sliding scale. The latter option means that the royalty rate increases as the book sales increase.

Would you get an advance on top of royalties?

No. An advance is your royalties paid up front. When a publisher pays an advance they're gambling that your book will sell, because instead of waiting to see how many copies sell and paying you once they have all the sales information, they give you a chunk of royalties before the book is even in the shops. If the book then fails to sell, they've lost out and you keep the advance. If you're paid a big advance for a book, you might never receive any more money for that book unless it earns enough to bring your account with the publisher back into credit.

Would you get royalties for the rest of your life?

It's possible, in theory, but not many books prove to be so durable. The average lifespan for a printed book is three years. Bookshops are under daily pressure to create shelf space for new titles, so they are constantly updating the range of titles they keep in stock. But with the advent of new book technologies such as eBooks it's possible that the royalties could stream in forever. There is unlimited shelf space in a cyberstore, so there's no reason for your book to cease existence after a few years (unless it is fundamentally out of date with regards its content).

Typical sales graph

Sales per month

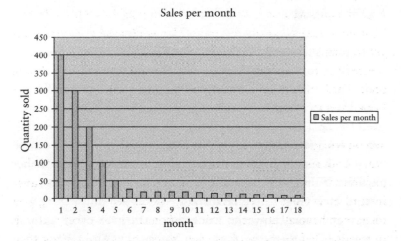

241

Bestseller sales graph

Sales per month

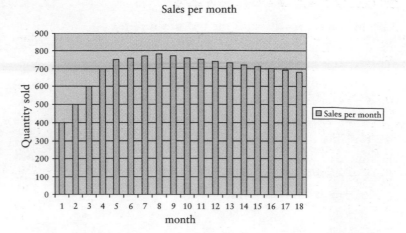

Fixed fees

Some publishers and producers don't pay royalties – they pay a fixed fee to a writer. This is common in journalism and for books and other media where the writing itself is generally not considered to be a major work. The kind of writing that attracts a fixed fee, be it article or book or script, is sometimes a work that only takes a few days to complete. But even longer works can be bought out for a fee. It's up to the writer to negotiate for a higher fixed fee if they feel the work is worth it, or to hold out for a royalty deal. There's no guarantee the publisher will be prepared to pay any more, however, since they may have other authors prepared to do the same work for that money. When a fixed fee is paid there will never be any other income for the author for that writing because all rights to the work are purchased by the publisher or producer.

Are there others ways to earn money from a book?

Many potential ways exist, though it's rare for all of them to come to fruition. The possible extra incomes are:

Translation editions
Foreign publishers pay your publisher for the right to translate and publish the book in their language. You would receive a portion of this money. In theory a book can sell to dozens of different publishers around the world. I've had my books translated into Chinese, Hungarian, Italian, Portuguese, Spanish, Dutch and other languages.

Other English-language editions
This could result from a publisher in another English-speaking country buying the right to publish in that country, or from a company in your own country wishing to publish a different version, such as a large-print edition or a book-club edition. I've had English-language editions published in Australia, India and America as well as the UK.

Extract and serial rights
Newspapers and magazines sometimes pay publishers for the right to print extracts from a book. I've even been paid by an examination board which used an extract from one of my books in an English comprehension test.

Audio rights
A company may buy the rights to record your book for an audio edition either for sale or broadcast.

Film rights

Hundreds of film rights to books are purchased every year. Not all make it to the big screen, but the writer of the original book gets paid nonetheless.

Television rights

Many television series started life in book form. Detective novels seem to transfer from page to screen particularly well.

eBook sales

This is a growing market sector that provides an extra revenue stream for publishers and authors and eBook rights are now a significant part of any publishing deal. Royalty rates for eBooks are often higher than for print editions.

Personal appearances

When an author makes a name for themselves they can charge for after-dinner speaking, masterclasses, coaching and interviews with the press, radio and television. I've made more than fifty television appearances as an author and publisher, and every show either paid me well for my time or allowed me to plug my books on the show in order to boost sales.

Merchandising

No one's yet made an offer to produce plastic dolls in my likeness, but if they did my publishing contracts would have a clause to cover that eventuality. Merchandising is important in children's publishing when characters become popular enough to warrant the production of lunchboxes, games, branded clothes and other items featuring those characters.

Top tips on copyright, agents, contracts and royalties

- Keep all of your notes and drafts and deleted text in case you ever need it to prove you wrote something.
- If you can persuade an agent to sign you up, your work will be considered by larger companies with deeper pockets, but it's not easy finding an agent who will take on a new writer.
- Publishing contracts appear to be weighted in favour of the publisher in terms of the division of income, but this is necessary in order to pay for the expenses associated with printing and selling books.
- Most print books only sell for a few years, whereas eBooks have an indefinite shelf life.

❝ *If you want to be a writer, you must do two things above all others: read a lot and write a lot.* **❞**

STEPHEN KING

THE NEXT STEP

Writing is one of those professions – like acting and pop music – in which more people want to make a living out of it than the industry is able to support. Those holding the purse strings can therefore afford to be fussy. Publishers, agents and producers can and do pick only the best. Mediocre writing isn't good enough. Even good writing often isn't good enough. To be a successful writer takes greatness, and greatness is the natural by-product of dedicating yourself to your creativity. It comes from making the transition from being someone who writes to being a Writer. And I think the capital 'W' is significant because the word Writer needs to define you. It is what you are from the moment you wake up to the moment you sleep. Hopefully it will sometimes continue in your dreams, too, resolving problems and seeding new ideas, scenes and characters ready for you to develop the next day.

Ready to begin your transformation into a Writer? Start now. Give your writing the care and diligence and sheer effort it deserves. Set a low, achievable word count as your minimum daily target (say 250 words), and get it done today. Get it done tomorrow. Keep up that routine all of this week and into the next. Aim for thirty days of unbroken progress with your writing.

Refer back to the chapters on inspiration and writer's block when you need to, but don't let anything hold you back. Keep going. Maintaining enthusiasm, self-belief and a steadily expanding text document are crucial. What you write in those thirty days may just be a diary or pages of a book that will never be published or a very rough first draft of something that will need copious amounts of reworking afterwards, but it doesn't matter. It's part of the transition process that will turn you into what you want to be.

If you fail to achieve your word target on one of the days, for any reason, there is a small penance: you reset the clock and start the count towards thirty days of continuous output again. Keep resetting it whenever you slip up, because when you finally get to the thirtieth continuous day of writing, something wonderful is going to happen… you're going to keep on writing. Don't stop. Make this your habit, your lifestyle, your love affair.

Don't strive for money, strive for perfection. Don't think of writing as a chore, think of it as a passion. Most writers settle for mediocre. Some settle for good. Push yourself to be better than them and you'll have eliminated 90 per cent of the competition and put yourself on the fast track to success.

DEFINITIONS

Advance
An amount of royalties paid to a writer before the product is released.

Blog
A 'web log', or online diary. It's like having your own newspaper column from which you can dissipate your opinions to the world.

Blurb
The short description of a book that is usually printed on the back cover or in the jacket sleeve.

Draft
A stage in the creation of a written work which may appear to be complete, but which requires further work (culminating in the final draft).

eBook
Downloadable, electronic version of a book. Various digital formats exist, some of which look the same as the print edition, while others more closely resemble web pages with text that flows to fill the available screen size.

Edit
A process of improving a written work from the point of view of spelling, grammar, facts, structure, style and length. Although this is done by publishers it's important for authors to do as much of this as possible before submitting their work for consideration.

DEFINITIONS

ISBN
International Standard Book Number. This identifies every edition of every book to enable efficient ordering and stock control in the bookstores.

Manuscript
Literally means a handwritten book, but the word is in general use today to mean any unpublished work whether typed or in a word-processed format.

Royalty
A payment made to an author based on sales quantity or sales income.

Submission
Typically a covering letter, synopsis and a couple of sample chapters submitted to a publisher.

Synopsis
A summary of a book or other written work, usually not much more than a page in length.

Typescript
Refers to an unpublished book in typed form, although usually synonymous with 'manuscript'.

USEFUL WEBSITES
AND SOFTWARE

There are links to websites and organisations, other books and some great writing software (some of which is free) on my website that can help you to launch your writing career in any direction you choose. Just visit www.stewartferris.com for these links. You'll also find some very useful free downloads that I've made available, plus updates for this book and links to other titles in this series.

NOTES

_____
_____
_____
_____
_____
_____
_____
_____
_____
_____
_____
_____
_____
_____
_____
_____
_____
_____

NOTES

<u>NOTES</u>

HOW TO GET PUBLISHED

Secrets from the Inside

Stewart Ferris

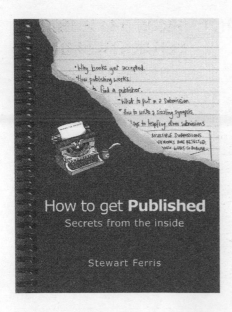

Paperback

£5.99

ISBN: 978-1-84024-438-0

The concept that a good book will always find a publisher is outdated and over-simplistic. The sad truth is that most writers remain unpublished because they pay attention only to the quality of their writing. Publishers are business people. Their job is to make money from selling books. They know that high quality writing alone isn't always enough to make a profitable book, so when choosing which manuscripts to sign up for publication they think about many more elements than just the words on the page.

After 20 years in the book industry, Stewart Ferris has identified all of the crucial factors that publishers consider besides good writing. *How to Get Published* reveals for the first time these inside secrets and provides tactics that any writer can use to create the perfect conditions for their own 'lucky break' to happen.

HOW TO PUBLISH YOUR OWN BOOK

Secrets from the Inside

Stewart Ferris

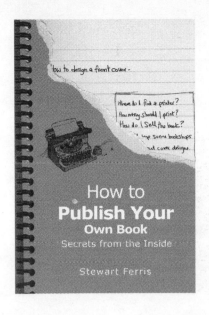

Paperback

£6.99

ISBN: 978-1-84024-519-6

When you've written a book you want to see it in print. You want people to read and enjoy it. The only thing standing in your way is the publishing industry, which rejects 98 per cent of the manuscripts submitted to it. Why not skip months of collecting rejections from publishers and join them at their own game? Anyone can publish their own book, and the cost can be as little as zero.

In this easy-to-use guide, Stewart Ferris explains everything you need to know to be able to convert your manuscript into a printed book and to get that book selling in the shops, or to sell it online as an eBook.

Have you enjoyed this book?

If you're interested in finding out more about our books,
follow us on Twitter: **@Summersdale**

Thanks very much for buying this Summersdale book.

www.summersdale.com